Praise for *You Can Retire Sooner Than You Think*

"I love, love, love this book. Wes Moss has knocked it out of the park. So many people are intimidated by saving for retirement, spending in retirement, and living in retirement. Wes deals with all three of these concerns with plain-talking good sense backed by rock solid research. The goal is to be happy, not rich.

"The keys that Wes identifies to having a happy retirement are simple but brilliant. Read this book."

—CLARK HOWARD, consumer advocate,
nationally syndicated radio talk show host,
and author of *Clark Howard's Living Large in Lean Times*

"*You Can Retire Sooner Than You Think* is the modern day version of *The Millionaire Next Door*—it gives you an honest guide to an early and happy retirement. Through his national survey on money and happiness, Wes Moss discovered a groundbreaking answer to the question 'Can money buy happiness?' and in this book he gives you the steps to retire early and happy. This book is packed with great advice regardless of your age or financial situation."

—ANDY DEAN, nationally syndicated radio host
of *America Now with Andy Dean*

YOU CAN
RETIRE
SOONER
THAN YOU
THINK

YOU CAN RETIRE SOONER THAN YOU THINK

The 5 Money Secrets of the Happiest Retirees

WES MOSS

Mc
Graw
Hill
Education

New York   Chicago   San Francisco   Athens   London   Madrid
Mexico City   Milan   New Delhi   Singapore   Sydney   Toronto

1 2 3 4 5 6 7 8 9 0   DOC/DOC   1 2 0 9 8 7 6 5 4

ISBN   978-0-07-183902-0
MHID   0-07-183902-X

e-ISBN   0-07-183903-8
e-MHID   978-0-07-183903-7

Library of Congress Cataloging-in-Publication Data
Moss, Wes.
   You can retire sooner than you think / by Wes Moss.
      pages cm
   ISBN 978-0-07-183902-0 (paperback : alk. paper) — ISBN 0-07-183902-X
(alk. paper) 1. Retirement—Planning. 2. Finance, Personal. I. Title.
   HQ1062.M657 2014
   332.024'014—dc23

                                                                2014010570

McGraw-Hill Education books are available at special quantity discounts to use as premiums and sales promotions or for use in corporate training programs. To contact a representative, please visit the Contact Us pages at www .mhprofessional.com.

This book is dedicated with love
to my wife, Lynne,
and three sons,
Ben, Luke, and Jake.

Contents

PART ONE

The Happy Retiree Basics

PART FOUR

Enjoying the Rest of Your Life

Foreword

I try so hard to get my listeners and viewers to save for a rainy day and save for retirement. You may intend to do both, but life somehow gets in the way. Even if you have a mind to save, most of us find saving money intimidating. It is confusing to know how much to save, where to save it, what kind of investments to have, and who to trust.

I believe that you should start with a map: where are you trying to go? I know a guy who plays the lottery twice per week. He dreams of being the winner of one of those mega jackpots. I asked him what he would do if he won. His answer, "I won't be at work tomorrow." Then I asked him what he would do with his life after he stopped working. I was met with a blank stare.

Retirement or not working is fine, but only if you have a plan for doing what you enjoy, how you would spend your days, and what your ideal life would cost. Then you can start to set goals.

My 67-year-old brother Gary is a retired lawyer. He spends his days volunteering, and he and his wife take about a trip a month to see the United States and the world.

Gary and his wife Debra began planning 20 years ago. They hired a fee-only financial planner. The planner did what any great planner will do. He asked what they enjoyed and what their dreams were. He then estimated what that lifestyle would cost and how much they would have to save to make it happen by the time my brother was 65. Debra has decided not to retire yet and is still working full time, which has made my brother's transition to retirement easier.

But it isn't just about dollars and cents. Retirement should be a joy. As you read this book, you will learn the keys to having a happy retirement. You might think that happiness is strictly personal. What would make you happy is completely different from what would make me happy. However, you will be surprised and ultimately convinced that certain traits and steps are common if you want real, lasting happiness when your workdays sail into the sunset.

Wes Moss uses his many years of experience as an investment advisor to real-life families to create a must-read for you if you want to retire happy. He has facts and many of the important keys that lead to true happiness as work goes into the rear-view mirror.

Wes unlocks the secrets to a happy retirement.

Clark Howard
Nationally syndicated talk show host,
consumer advocate, and author of
Clark Howard's Living Large in Lean Times

Preface

Does Money
Buy Happiness?

'Ve kept very few mementos in my life—only a handful—and most have been lost over time. But there's one movie ticket stub I've held onto for the last eight years.

I keep it in the same little wooden box that holds my watch and my wedding ring—the same little wooden box I open every morning as I'm getting ready for work. So I see the ticket nearly every morning of my life . . . and I've been looking at it since the movie came out in 2006.

The Pursuit of Happyness.

I have three young sons myself, so the story really resonated with me. Every time I even *think* about complaining about the financial industry or the lackluster performance of a particular stock, I remember the story of Chris Gardner (played by Will Smith) who was homeless and taking care of his five-year-old son as he began what would eventually become a successful career as an investment advisor.

All this to say, I guess I've always put extreme importance on being happy—and trying to help others do the same.

So how do we get happy? Do we have to do what Chris Gardner did and start pulling a six-figure income? Is that what it's all about?

Even as a kid, I was intrigued by the relationship between money and happiness. I've spent my whole life asking the question: Does money buy happiness? It's still the number one question I am asked when I do radio and TV interviews: What's the link between money and happiness? Do you need loads of the first to get more of the second?

We all ask those questions. Every one of us is familiar with the nagging questions: "Do I have enough? Will I go broke?" And the one place in our lives where those questions really crystallize is when we start thinking about retirement. Talk about a landscape where people's biggest dreams collide with the harshest realities!

We want to retire early, but we're not sure we can. We have big plans for the future, but we don't know if we can afford them. We long to see the world, but we don't know when we'll be able to stop working—and we're too scared to find out.

My entire career has been devoted to helping people retire as soon as they possibly can. I do it every day at CIA (no, not the Central Intelligence Agency—in my case it stands for my firm, Capital Investment Advisors). I've helped hundreds of couples and individuals retire sooner—and more comfortably—than they ever thought possible. How do I do it? Naturally, we put financial strategies in place and rely on specific investment vehicles and tools. But there's something else, too, something bigger going on.

I'll tell you my secret: **If you want to retire early, you have to figure out the relationship between money and happiness.** I truly believe this is the key—and it has the power to unlock the retirement of your dreams.

This isn't the sort of stuff you hear investment advisors talk about. Most people in the world of finance are far more comfortable chatting about stocks and bonds than discussing the nebulous, feel-good concept of "happy." But not me. I love talking about this stuff. I talk about it all the time when hosting *Money Matters*, one of the most widely listened to and longest-running personal finance and investment radio shows in the United States. And, thanks to my radio audience and a healthy client list, I have access to one of the most extensive pools of retirees in the nation.

You'd better believe I make good on it. Using the world's most popular and robust online survey tool, I conducted a comprehensive study of more than 1,350 retirees across 46 states. I asked my survey participants more than three dozen questions on a variety of topics: income history, their assets, home value and level of mortgage debt, spending habits, sense of purpose, how many vacations they took, what kind of cars they drove, and where they went out for dinner—just to name a few. Some of my findings were exactly what I'd suspected; others weren't.

This book is the culmination of that journey, the result of all the studying and testing and researching I have done on my quest to figure out: Does money buy happiness? And more specifically: Does money buy happiness in retirement?

I've been asking those questions all my life.

The answers, of course, are far from simple: it does, and it doesn't.

It Does

At its most fundamental level, money provides three things: safety, health, and freedom. No one can argue that your retirement income will provide:

- Safety. One of the greatest fears people face is running out of money. I hear it all the time: "I don't want to be broke." "I don't want to have to depend on my kids to take care of me." Once we reach a certain level of net worth and have obtained a "cushion," we can take these basic human fears off the table. What a relief! You'll no longer spend sleepless nights worried about running out of money and being forced out on the street, or fretting over not being able to buy groceries. It's a direct link: a certain level of money equates a certain level of safety.

- **Health.** There are certainly no guarantees that money will equal good health; plenty of millionaires die young, victims to cancer or other debilitating diseases (think Steve Jobs). However, having a financial cushion and a certain level of resources will ensure that if something does go wrong medically, you will have the best chance of getting the treatment and medical attention you need.
- **Freedom.** Once our basic needs are covered (food, shelter, health), money provides an additional benefit: the ability to *enjoy* the fruits of our labor. This freedom takes different forms for different people: it could be traveling, going to the opera, playing volleyball, spending time with grandkids, or volunteering at a favorite charity.

And It Doesn't

But here's what you may not know: money buys happiness *only to a certain point*. After a certain level of wealth is achieved, a "plateau effect" occurs, resulting in a diminishing return on happiness.

In America, we tend to have a sense of what our standard of living *should* look like. Once we get there, we've essentially achieved our goals. The funny thing is, the more we add on from that point, the less it affects our overall well-being.

The Woodrow Wilson School at Princeton University recently conducted a study showing that once people reach an income in the neighborhood of $75,000 per year, happiness levels off.[1] In other words, your chances of avoiding unhappiness are greater if you make at least $75,000 per year, but you don't keep getting happier and happier from there. I call this "diminishing marginal happiness."

Yes, more income and more "cushion" get us to a point where we can enjoy greater safety and the freedom to pursue the things we love. But once we get to a certain point, we are often able to "buy and do everything that I ever wanted to do"—to borrow a line from one of my favorite happy retirees.

It's all in the data—I'm not making this up. It's as if, once we have a cushion, *more money doesn't necessarily add to our sense of how great that cushion really is.*

I want you to keep that in mind as you read this book. Retiring early is not about saving as much money as you possibly can. Of course, you want to have a cushion that affords safety, freedom, and a better chance of staying healthy, and saving and investing your money wisely matters—I'd be crazy to say otherwise. But it's also about the life you've been building for yourself, the choices you make, and the activities you pursue.

The happiest retirees know this. They're happy not just because they have money in the bank, or because they know the five money secrets: they're happy because they are living with purpose—whatever "purpose" means for them.

If you want to know *how* they do it—if you want to follow in the footsteps of the thousands of men and women who have been able to retire early and retire happy—then keep reading. I wrote this book for you.

Introduction

How to Read This Book

Here's a sobering statistic: 75 percent of Americans nearing retirement age have less than $30,000 in their retirement accounts. That's right—*less than thirty thousand bucks*. That's enough for one really nice family vacation, maybe, or a new roof, but nowhere near enough to guarantee the safety, health, and freedom a financial cushion could (and should) provide.

This is 75 percent of U.S. citizens we're talking about. What kind of retirement do you think these people are headed toward? An unhappy one, I'll bet.

I don't want you to be one of those people. We hear a lot today about the "1 percent," but I'm talking about a different percentage: I want you to be one of the 25 percent. I want you to have way more than $30,000 in the bank. More important: **I want to help you pave the way for a retirement that is infinitely more fun, thrilling, and fulfilling than you ever dreamed.**

There are plenty of books on how to retire happy, and there are plenty of books on how to retire rich. I want to show you how to retire *early*—and how to be happier than all your friends and family who are still toiling away at their nine to five.

Retiring early and happy isn't only about the money in your accounts. Sure, money is important—I won't deny it. But the happiest retirees know it's about so much more than their bottom line. It's not necessarily about having the most money; it's about your outlook on life and the choices you make. It's about using your money as the means to reach your purpose, not the other way around.

This book is about money and happiness, and how to arrive at that intersection as soon as humanly possible. I've helped hundreds of retirees retire earlier than they thought they'd be able to, and now I want to do the same for you. I'm going to take you through the process step-by-step to make sure you're on the right track.

You could be 35 or 60—it doesn't matter. The advice in this book works for anyone thinking about retirement, whether you're retiring next week or you have 30 years to go. And if you're headed for troubled waters, it is not too late to turn the ship around. I've had people come to me who were practically bankrupt, both financially and emotionally, and within a few years of hard work and smart choices, we were able to completely change the course of their future. I know what works and what doesn't. I'm familiar with the myths people buy into and the common traps that ensnare them.

In these pages I'll be giving you five critically important money secrets that will lead to retirement as soon as possible, but what I'm really giving you are the secrets behind how the happiest retirees got happy—and how they stayed that way.

In Part One we'll talk about the happy retiree basics. I'll introduce you to some of my favorite happy retirees—as well as some preretirees who are well on their way to retiring ahead of schedule. We'll talk about the life and money choices these people made to get them where they are today. We'll also look at some unhappy retirees and how you can avoid making the same mistakes.

Part Two will focus on the top five money secrets of the happiest retirees—the five inviolable financial strategies you need to adhere to. We'll look at:

- **Secret #1:** Determine what you want and need your retirement money for.
- **Secret #2:** Figure out how much money you need to have saved before you retire.
- **Secret #3:** Pay off your mortgage in as little as five years.
- **Secret #4:** Develop an income stream from three or four sources, not just one.
- **Secret #5:** Become an income investor.

I'll spend one chapter on each of these secrets, providing tangible tools, action steps, and how-to lists to get you started. I'll also introduce you to a number of happy retirees who have put the five money secrets to excellent use.

In Part Three, I'll share my proven approach to successful long-term investing. I'll guide you through the process of minimizing risk and avoiding common pitfalls. Every investor is unique, and your portfolio should be unique, too: the mix of stocks, bonds, real estate, and cash should reflect both your risk tolerance and your specific financial goals. We'll talk about how to make the right choices and sidestep the bad ones.

And in Part Four, we'll zoom out a bit to look at the bigger picture. To get you excited about your retirement, I'll show you the vibrant world of opportunities available to you. Travel, service, golf, time spent with friends and family—it's all yours. Here we'll meet more fantastic people from the happy camp, and you'll see yourself in their stories: the many ways they are embracing and enjoying their rich and wonderful lives.

You bought this book because you want to retire early and happy. I can help you get there. In the chapters that follow, I've distilled the traits, strategies, and secrets of America's happiest retirees into easy-to-understand, actionable steps. No matter how long you have until your years turn golden, you can start moving toward a happy retirement today.

Sound good? Glad to hear it.

Get ready to get happy.

Acknowledgments

There's a significant team of people that I must thank for their insight, guidance, encouragement, support, and effort on this book project. And yes, this has been more than writing a book—this has been a research project on *money and happiness*, and how the two can work together to make an *early retirement* a reality for the reader. So, many thanks and in no particular order to a wonderful team:

The Money Matters Team—a beautiful group of people, aka Team CIA, at Capital Investment Advisors. They have supported this project for the nearly two years it took to complete. From idea, to survey research, to analyzing survey data, to formulating a road map on how this book would develop, Team CIA has been integral in the formulation of this book.

Countless hours were spent with Ryan Ely, also part of the CIA team and the producer of *Money Matters* Radio. A financial brain in his own right, I applaud his efforts in helping me flush out the stories this book was written to tell—and the advice it was meant to impart on our audience.

My "English Professor" and literary agent Cindy Zigmund—who has been instrumental in helping me focus on what is truly unique and most important about this work. She was the original believer in the book's message and has been a wonderful guide through this process.

Two of the best storytelling, content editing, and literary polishing partners on the planet—Ryan Doolittle and Bree Barton, who made this project memorable, and just plain fun from start to finish.

To the many clients and listeners that I interviewed for their unique story on how they were able to *retire sooner than they thought* possible. This book changes their names and minor details to protect their anonymity—but their real-world financial success has taught me volumes, and it will hopefully be passed on to you.

My wife Lynne and three young sons—who "let dad slide" for the time it took to finish this book. "Dad, are you done with your book yet? When are you are you going to *be done*?" I'm happy to report, we're here.

And to McGraw Hill—a publishing giant that has been kind enough to notice my work and the story I am trying to tell. Tom Miller—thank you for pushing this project beyond what I originally thought it could become.

YOU CAN
RETIRE
SOONER
THAN YOU
THINK

PART ONE

The Happy Retiree Basics

CHAPTER 1

Who Are the Happy Retirees, and What Makes Them Happy?

R *etire.*
Few words in the English language carry as much weight as this one.

In a baseball game, if a pitcher retires the side quickly, that means he shut the other team down. He's an ace! On the other hand, if the team retires his jersey, that jersey is no longer worn— it no longer functions. They hang it up in the rafters, or in a musty locker room that smells of sweat and dirty socks.

Even when I was young, I remember thinking retirement was a good thing. As far as I could tell, retirement meant you could just stop working, and that was good, right?

Or is it? When our heart stops working, we die. So what happens when we stop working?

Over time, as I've thought about this more, I've realized it's not really that we want to retire. It's that we want to be in the *position* to retire. There's a big difference. We don't want to stop working, but we do want to stop working with our annoying boss, or our lazy coworkers, pushy vendors, expensive lawyers, or demanding clients. We don't really want to stop everything and make shuffleboard or mah-jongg the highlight of the day. We just want to be in the financial position to not have to grind it out at a job we no longer love, or maybe never loved.

We want the option. We want the freedom. This is America!

As our economy has taken its lumps over the past decade, I've gotten the sense that more and more Americans view a happy retirement as an elusive or even unattainable goal. So they work harder, logging more hours and losing more sleep, striving tirelessly toward the notion of a happy retirement. Their logic is simple: work more, save more, be happier. Makes sense, right?

Wrong. It doesn't always work that way.

Today the paradigm has shifted. It's not always about working longer or harder; it's about making smart choices with your money and your life. Some of the old strategies still work, others don't—and you have to know what to keep and what to discard.

I'm here to tell you: you can create your own definition of retirement—and you can do it sooner than you think. I don't just want you to retire. I want you to retire *happy*. And now you can.

What Makes a Retiree Happy?

I don't claim to be a doctor of happiness, but I *do* claim to have done my research. In my comprehensive survey of more than 1,350 retirees across 46 states, I was ruthless in my quest for answers. I asked retirees the questions no one else was asking. Sure, I asked about net worth and income, total assets and home value. But I asked them other questions, too, about their overall quality of life.

First, I asked them: How happy would you rate yourself on a scale of 1 to 5, where 1 is not happy and 5 is extremely happy?

Then I invited them to tell me about their lives. Where did they shop? What kind of cars did they drive? How many vacations did they take each year? Were they married or divorced? Did they have children? If so, how many? What activities and interests did they pursue? How would they define their purpose in life?

Once the data was crunched, I went to the Georgia Tech Department of Mathematics and had the data's "confidence and significance" verified by the former president of the GA Tech Math Club, along with one of her former math professors. I used the data to create a series of graphs and charts, which you'll see throughout this book.

The more I looked at the survey data, the more things I found that surprised me. Happy retirees hate fast food and love steak. They avoid cheap chains but don't overindulge either—Ruth's Chris Steak House and Olive Garden rank among their favorite restaurants. They shop at Macy's and Kohl's. They don't drive BMWs, though unhappy retirees often do.

Happy retirees have busy social schedules. They play sports and volunteer, whereas unhappy retirees tend to prefer hunting and reading. They have at least two kids, and three seems to be the magic number. The happy folks have at least 3.5 *core pursuits*—the activities and interests they love to do. (More on core pursuits in Chapter 4.) And lest you think retirees are homebodies: take a look at Illustration 1.1. Happy retirees average 2.4 annual vacations, while retirees in the unhappy group take only 1.4. One vacation may not seem like a big deal, but it can mean the difference between being happy and being miserable.

In addition to the fun stuff, I pinpointed certain financial signifiers that showed up repeatedly among the happy retirees. They lived in homes with a value of at least $300,000. They didn't have a mortgage; if they did, their payoff was in sight. They had a liquid net worth of at least $500,000, and they spent at least five hours per year planning for retirement, usually more.

Illustration 1.1   Average Number of Vacations per Year

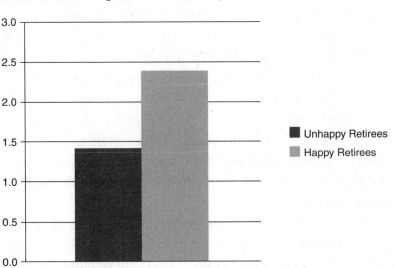

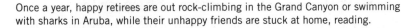

Once a year, happy retirees are out rock-climbing in the Grand Canyon or swimming with sharks in Aruba, while their unhappy friends are stuck at home, reading.

They also had at least two or three different sources of income in retirement, including social security, pension income, income from investments, income from rental properties, part-time work, and government benefits (Illustrations 1.2 and 1.3). In Chapter 7, we'll go into more depth on how having diverse sources of income can lead to greater happiness.

Have you noticed one theme that keeps repeating itself? **Overall, the happiest retirees live in the "middle."** When it comes to home values, vacations, restaurants, cars, and shopping, happy retirees have found the sweet spot in the middle. Nothing low-rent, but not high-end either. They're not spending lavishly—but they're also not depriving themselves. They've struck the balance that's right for them.

I'd like to help you strike the balance that's right for you.

On the 1-to-5 happiness scale, I want to see you at a 4 or 5. I want money to facilitate that happiness, not create it. Start

Illustration 1.2   Happy Retirees' Number of Income Sources

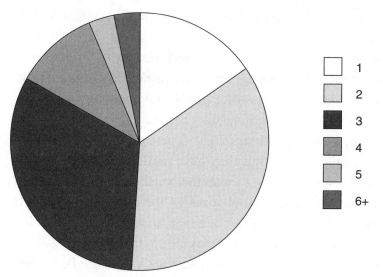

☐	1
☐	2
■	3
■	4
☐	5
■	6+

Illustration 1.3   Unhappy Retirees' Number of Income Sources

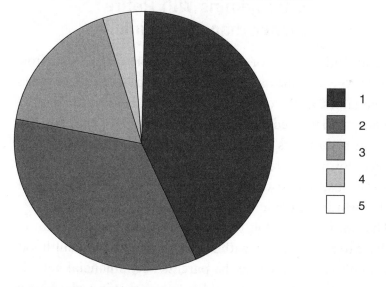

■	1
■	2
☐	3
☐	4
☐	5

The vast majority of happy retirees have two or three income sources, while the majority of unhappy retirees have one or two.

thinking of money as a way to *support* being happy, rather than manufacture it. If you can make that subtle shift, you're well on your way.

In the following pages, I'll introduce you to a number of happy retirees who have applied these principles with great success. I don't have to look far for people in the happy group—my client base is chock-full of them. These are people who, for the most part, have done things right. They're not all millionaires and multimillionaires, but they have made smart choices with their money and are able to reap the benefits.

I'll also introduce you to some of the families I work with who haven't retired yet. These are men and women in their thirties, forties, and fifties who are making smart decisions *now* that will pay off later. Take, for example, Nick and Katie Benjamin.

The Benjamins Will Retire Sooner than You Think

Nick and Katie are one of my favorite couples. Both come from parents whose retirements were completely crushed by their respective companies. Both vowed never to let that happen to them.

Katie's dad worked for Chicago Bridge & Iron. They laid him off a year prior to his full pension eligibility, so his pension got whacked down to 20 cents on the dollar. He didn't really have a 401(k) because that just wasn't a standard benefit during his era. In other words, he got a bum deal.

That means Katie felt the financial brunt as well. A lot of kids have to move back in with their parents early in adulthood, but it's not usually because the parents need financial help. In this case, Katie's parents needed her to pay rent in order to stay solvent on their mortgage!

Nick's dad worked for Eastern Air Lines, a big airline in Atlanta that went out of business in 1991. It took him a long time to find work again. Like Katie's dad, his pension got severely hit and he ended up with miniscule savings. Now, both of their parents are in their seventies and barely scraping by. Nick and Katie are going to have to help support them.

It's easy to see the genesis of a mentality that has taken hold in Nick and Katie. It's been apparent to me ever since they started working with me a decade ago. Their determination set them on a course of making razor-sharp financial decisions. It kept them from sinking money into a house they couldn't afford or cars they shouldn't drive. If they stay on course, Nick and Katie may be able to retire in their midfifties. Do I have your attention yet? Good.

Nick and Katie both work, and they each make around $150,000 to $175,000 a year. Not a bad chunk of change, especially in Atlanta. But they haven't always had this powerful double income—and they're certainly not one of the much-discussed "1 percent," which in 2011 required a minimum household income of $516,633. For many of their first years of marriage, they were both averaging around $75,000 a year, both as consultants in the technology industry. So despite their new relatively high double income, Nick still drives a 1995 Nissan Maxima with 200,000 miles on it. Katie drives a 1998 Nissan Maxima with 300,000 miles on it. They do have a used 2001 S-Class Mercedes, which is pretty nice but reasonable.

They aren't on financial lockdown, either. They aren't total stiffs. I wouldn't be writing about them if they were. They go out to dinner, they eat what they want, and don't have to worry about the little stuff because they know they are nailing it on the big fundamentals. **Because they are pound-wise, they can afford to be penny-foolish at times.**

The most important big-ticket item is their housing situation, and it almost didn't go in the right direction. Like many, Nick and Katie were at a crossroads and nearly took the wrong turn. They made a deposit on an expensive house that would've basically depressed them financially—for years if not decades. Everyone else was doing it. Why not them?

But then they thought long and hard about what they were doing. Taking a small penalty, they decided to get their deposit back on the house and instead live in a two-bedroom apartment for the next two to three years. They took that deposit ($30,000) and used it to pay down student debt.

That gave them the momentum to continue making smart choices. They began to live by a rule of maxing out their 401(k)s every year, no matter what. Though they were both bringing in salaries, they decided to live on just one salary—the lower of the two. They had vacation time, but kept it regional, often opting for the "staycation" to avoid huge out-of-pocket costs.

When I met Nick and Katie in 2004, right after I finished my run on NBC's *The Apprentice*, they were 34 and 32 years of age, respectively. They had $50,000 total in savings. Today they have over $450,000 in retirement assets saved. They own their own home, on which they owe less than $200,000 of its $250,000 value, and it will be paid off by the time Nick is 50 years old.

That's not all. They own seven single ranch home rental properties, all in the $100,000 to $150,000 range. Sure, they made a few mistakes along the way, such as buying a couple of houses right before the housing bubble burst in 2007. However, they learned from those mistakes. They were able to do some financing through a government program called HARP 2, which essentially gave them a way to refinance and get better interest rates even on some of their properties that were "underwater" (properties that were worth less than they owed). Submarine financing, if you will.

Nick and Katie lowered their interest rates, which stopped the bleeding that was their $1,800 a month of net negative cash flow. From there, they began to break even, and they then bought a couple of other smaller places in 2009 and 2010 that finally provided a positive cash flow.

The Benjamins will have their mortgage paid off by age 50, and they'll be able to do the things they want to do. They'll have a real purpose behind their money. Katie will work part-time in real estate without any pressure. She'll teach spin classes rather than just going to the gym. Nick will play more golf. They will travel more. They are currently pregnant, having decided to have a child later in life. Since my studies have shown that the more kids you have (up to three), the happier you are, this was music to my ears.

Nick and Katie lived and still live slightly below their means, which is key. We all know how to do it, but we get caught with our hands in the consumer cookie jar. Ever since the days of "Mad Men" in the 1950s, marketing campaigns in America have been extremely adept at convincing Americans to buy whatever they want to buy. Madison Avenue has made us feel financially invincible.

We aren't.

But if we live like the Benjamins, we don't have to be. With judicious decisions and hard work, you too can retire early. You don't need $5 million to do it. You may not even need $1 million. The Benjamins have less than half of that (though they're well on their way to having a good deal more). Thanks to their singular focus and smart financial choices, they're on track to retiring a lot sooner than their friends and coworkers.

Wouldn't you like that to be you?

5 Action Steps Toward an Early Retirement

The Benjamins are the kind of people who take action; it's just the way they live their lives. So, inspired by Nick and Katie, here are five action steps *you* can take. These steps will move you that much closer to retiring early—just like the Benjamins will be doing in a few years.

1. **Keep your primary monthly mortgage payments (as a percentage of your income) well below the conventional "25 to 30 percent of your monthly income."** If possible, aim for somewhere closer to 10 or 15 percent. Using the conventional "30 percent" rule that mortgage brokers will tell you, the Benjamins could "afford" a monthly mortgage payment of more than $7,000 a month. Instead, they pay less than $2,000 (or less than 10 percent of their taxable income) per month for their primary mortgage, including taxes and insurance.

2. **Pay your mortgage off early.** Using the above technique can give you plenty of room to make additional payments each month so your primary mortgage will be paid off early. Bankrate.com has a wonderful mortgage payment calculator section that allows you to see how $100 or more per month added to your mortgage payments can trim years off the overall life of the loan.

3. **Live on one of two incomes.** If you are a couple where both of you work, try to live on only one of the incomes. The Benjamins were able to live off the lower of the two, saving the majority of the rest—which also allowed them to start their mini–real estate empire. Even if you can't live on the lower of the two, living on the higher income and saving the entire lower income amount is still a wonderful practice.

4. **Forget about saving 10 percent a year.** It's a great start, but it just won't cut it—and it certainly won't allow you to retire early. I dedicate an entire section in this book (in Chapter 5) to something called taxes, saving, and life, where I'll show you the importance of saving at least 20 percent of your annual income.

5. **Start thinking about your future income.** If you know you
   will have some level of pension income, and social security,
   and investment income—great. But if you are like most
   Americans, you won't have a pension from the company
   you work for. In addition to the income your investment and
   retirement accounts will provide to you, consider buying
   income-producing properties like the Benjamins did. I
   suggest you aim in the $100,000 range to get started—
   maybe start small with a single-level ranch or condo. Once
   the mortgage is paid off, you'll have an asset that may be
   able to pay you nearly $10,000 a year in income. Talk about
   raking in some Benjamins!

CHAPTER 2

What Makes Retirees Unhappy—and How Can You Avoid It?

On a recent episode of my radio show, *Money Matters*, Chuck from Roswell called our listener line. He had just finished breakfast with his wife, and he was phoning in from the road. "Wes, I'm two years away from retirement. I'm driving a BMW 528i, and my wife is sitting next to me, saying, 'You need to get rid of this car.'"

He was laughing. You could hear his wife in the background, nudging him.

"Let's say I *do* want to be the happiest retiree," Chuck said. "What kind of car should I buy? My wife wants me to get a nice Toyota. In my heart, I know she's probably right. But what kind of cars do the happy people drive?"

"I'm so glad you called."

I had plenty of advice for Chuck—a whole list of the financial laws of happiness—the things that made retirees either happy or unhappy.

"Do you really want to be happy, Chuck?" I asked. "Then trade the BMW in for a Lexus. If you want kids, have three of them. And you need to take at least two vacations this year: Learn how to enjoy your money, or you're headed for the unhappy camp."

You can't control the economy, and you can't always avoid health scares or changes in circumstance. But there are things you *can* control, from small to big: everything from the kind of car you drive to the amount of money you put into savings each month. Why not start now?

In this chapter, we'll look at the financial choices and behaviors that lead to unhappiness. Most unhappy retirees don't even know they're headed for disaster; they have no idea how small, seemingly innocuous choices can add up to big financial ruin. Lucky for Chuck, he was able to change course before it was too late. His first mistake?

That sleek and shiny 528i.

Ditch the BMW and Stick to the Asian Brands

If you are retired and drive a BMW, chances are you are *not* happy. My survey results found that BMWs are the top luxury car in unhappy retirees' garages across America. My guess? The Chucks of the world are still competing. They buy the "Ultimate Driving Machine" because they're looking for a distraction—a high-end status symbol to make them feel better about themselves. But in purchasing such a car, they have opted, either knowingly or unknowingly, to add an additional financial burden to their lives.

It isn't that driving a luxury car leads to unhappiness. There are plenty of non-BMW luxury cars listed for the happy group. Their preferred luxury brands are Lexus and Buick; they tend to prefer Asian luxury brands by a three-to-one ratio. Happy retirees are looking for two things in the cars they drive: *comfort* and *cushion.* Anything else is just a well-polished money sump.

We did a five-year average cost comparison between Lexus and BMW, and the gap was significant: over five years, the average cost of owning a Lexus is *16 percent cheaper* than owning a BMW. Lexus is hardly considered the performance luxury brand, but retirees in the happy group don't seem all that interested in speed and handling when it comes to luxury automobiles.

I'm not saying owning a Lexus will automatically make you happy, just like owning a BMW won't automatically make you unhappy. All I'm saying is, after the top four makes of cars—GM, Ford, Honda, and Toyota—these are the cars that happy retirees drive. I'm guessing that's no coincidence.

The Happy Cars

- Lexus
- Nissan
- Hyundai
- Subaru
- Buick

The Happy Luxury Cars

- Lexus
- Buick
- Lincoln
- Mercedes

If you want to know what the unhappy retirees are driving (so you can avoid their fate), you should familiarize yourself with the Unhappy Cars: Chrysler, Dodge, Kia, Mercury, and of course, BMW.

You Don't Need a Second Career as a Stock Trader

I can't tell you how many unhappy retirees I've met who decide to "play the market." Now that they're no longer working, they have more time on their hands than ever before, so they think they'll become investment experts and active stock traders overnight.

Big mistake.

I have a client who is a semiretired radiologist. We'll call him Doctor Ray Gamma. Once Dr. Gamma saw the retirement light at the end of the tunnel, he began to scale back at the hospital. He went from working 80-hour weeks and 2 a.m. shifts to having more and more free time. He started burning the midnight oil poring over *Barron's* and *Bloomberg* instead.

Don't get me wrong—I love *Barron's*—but it can be dangerous to read without a solid context in financial planning. Dr. Gamma lacks essential financial context, for obvious reasons. He's not a financial planner; he's a semiretired doctor. He's constantly trying to redo and upgrade a plan that was put in place for him a year ago because he read about a hot new stock online. "Energy! Why don't I have more energy? Energy is the *it* buy!" "Biotechs! This biotech stock has a 14 percent yield—why don't we load up on this?"

What Dr. Gamma doesn't know is that last week the "it" buy was commodities, and the week before that it was semiconductors. There is always something "better" that you missed, something else you "could have" done—and 10 days after that it will be something else.

Is that how you want to live your life day to day? If so, the gods of unhappy retirement applaud you. Happy retirees know how to avoid the coulda-shoulda-woulda. Some are able to do this on their own, while others find an expert or advisor they can trust who will do this for them.

Dr. Gamma is hardworking and driven, but he's no expert in financial matters, just like I'm no expert in radiology. I would never tell Dr. Gamma how to perform his radiologist duties because it's not my field. So then why does he think he knows what's best for his own portfolio? I see it all the time, especially with retirees who were masters in their respective fields and assume they'll be equally gifted at managing their own money. They're smart people, but they're out of their depth. Unless you had a past life as a financial advisor, I'm betting the same applies to you.

If you're constantly tweaking your algorithms, frantically receiving Google alerts about the highest dividend-paying stocks, or making major investment choices because you read an obscure article in the *Wall Street Journal*, chances are you're going to end up disappointed. I encourage you to develop your own investment game plan that you can stick to or seek the counsel of a fee-only investment advisor that will help you do so.

Give Your Money a Purpose

For many unhappy retirees, the only purpose of having money in retirement is to have money in retirement. Happy retirees, on the other hand, know their money is merely the means for living a happy life, not the end goal.

I am constantly surprised and delighted by the many ways happy retirees define the purpose of their money. There are some who want to see the world and others who want to stay right here at home, getting more involved in their communities. There are those with a heart for service, people who want to earmark money for their favorite charities and philanthropies, and others who get excited about sending their grandkids off to college. The kind of legacy you leave is entirely up to you—but here are some possible ideas to get you excited.

- **Get active in a local charity that rings true to your heart.** You can get involved in a variety of ways:

raising awareness, fund-raising, recruiting people to the charity's events, serving on the board or on the committee for a program, or just rolling up your sleeves donating your time and energy. It's all good.

- **Open your own charitable gifting account, also known as a donor-advised fund.** You don't need millions of dollars to do this. Fidelity has a program called the Fidelity Charitable: you can start with an account for as little as $5,000. You choose your investment options, and each year, Fidelity will help you gift your desired amount to the nonprofit organizations you care about most. It's tax-deductible, and the company has even created a smartphone app that lets you contribute with the swipe of a finger. How easy is that? Head to www .fidelitycharitable.org for more info.

- **Explore crowdfunding organizations.** This is becoming a popular way for nonprofits and local community-based projects to find funding. In 2013, Atlanta-based Uruut proposed a plan to build a brand-new park and amphitheater for children. Once word got out, hundreds of small donations poured in over a matter of weeks. Ultimately, its crowdfunding website took in *over $100,000* and they were able to build the park. Research crowdfunding opportunities in your community, find a project you believe in, and pitch in.

Don't Move and Don't Renovate

These are two common traps for unhappy retirees. It makes sense, if you think about it: finally you have money and spare time on your hands. "It's about time," you tell your spouse. "Now we can finally do those home renovations we've been talking about for years!"

I advise you *not* to take this path. Consider Ron and Marie Carlyle, both 65 years old, a nice enough couple looking forward to a pleasant, peaceful retirement. But the Carlyles made a couple of critical mistakes, landing them squarely in the unhappy camp. They wanted to start their retirement off with a bang, so they sold their house and moved into a nice new place. Mistake #1: **Never make a big move at the beginning of retirement.** Sure, they had a nice new place, but they also had a nice new mortgage.

So there they were, in a new house with a lot of time on their hands. But guess what? The floor wasn't right for Marie. None of her old furniture worked at the new place. Consequently, Ron and Marie have spent the last two years adding a new floor, redoing the interior decorating, and buying new curtains, new furniture, and a brand-new kitchen. Of course, if you're going to redo the kitchen, you have to redo the bathroom, and if you redo the bathroom, you might as well redo the closet. See where I'm going with this? Mistake #2: **Now is not the time for costly renovations. Each one engenders one more.**

The Carlyles now have a massive financial outlay. They learned the hard way that home improvement is a slippery slope: it quickly starts to feel like a retiree's full-time job. Ron and Marie will either be forced to take on new debt—Mistake #3—or eat into a significant chunk of the very nest egg that was supposed to last in perpetuity. They spent all those years building a nest egg that they now have to crack wide open to make a home improvement omelet—an omelet that is going to taste like broken dreams.

If you get the itch to move or renovate, try following these two simple rules instead:

- **If you know you want to do some home improvements, the better strategy is to take care of it *before* you stop working.** Even if you save nothing in the last year or two of your career, that's still far better than using

$30,000 of your savings (or more) for a new kitchen and $20,000 of your nest egg for new hardwood floors.

- **If you'd like to move, try to take care of that before retirement as well.** Get settled during the last of your working years, rather than embarking on that journey while your retirement is embarking on you.

Make Big-Ticket Purchases *Before* You Retire

Unhappy retirees are prone to making big purchases, and worse, making them at precisely the wrong times. Happy retirees have a much healthier relationship to spending. It's not that they don't spend money. It's that they know when to do it: when they're still drawing a paycheck.

One of the advantages of retirement is being able to control both your cash flow and your taxes. Let's say when you're working, you're making $100,000 to $200,000 per year, which puts you in a really high tax bracket. As you move into retirement and begin to live on $60,000 to $70,000 per year, your tax bracket plummets accordingly, meaning you get to keep more of every dollar you make.

But if you take money out of your IRA for big-ticket purchases, you're raising your overall level of taxable income—and digging yourself deeper into the hole.

Take Lisa Hudson. Until very recently, Lisa was a happy retiree, but lately she's been hankering for a new boat to take out on the lake. She originally thought it was going to cost $10,000, but the latest estimate was closer to $20,000.

She said to me, "Wes, how much do I need to take out of my IRA in order to net $20,000?"

The answer is $25,000. Lisa has to withhold, on average, 15 percent for her federal taxes and 5 percent for state taxes (your state taxes may differ). So, that 20 percent gets taken off the top.

Again, money drawn from an IRA counts as income, so Lisa will be penalized for using money she's saved. If Lisa just had to have a boat to cruise into retirement, she should have bought it while she was still working.

The same rule applies if you're thinking of buying:

- A new car (not a BMW)
- A new central air system
- A new roof
- A new "toy" (boat, RV, Jet Ski, Harley, etc.)
- Any other large, one-time purchase

I'm not saying don't spend money on this stuff. I'm saying do it while you're still drawing a paycheck. You'll be happy you did.

Plan and Budget for Your Retirement

My survey results were clear about this: 44 percent of the unhappy group reported that they were "Not Satisfied" with the amount of retirement planning they had done, compared to only 3 percent of the happy group (Illustrations 2.1 and 2.2).

Almost all happy retirees have done their homework: they're enjoying their retirement because they *planned* to enjoy it. They did adequate legwork and preparation to ensure their reality would match their expectations. Unhappy retirees, on the other hand, just don't take the time. Here's a scary statistic: **Less than half of Americans plan for retirement at all.** That's right: Only 46 percent of workers have even tried to calculate what they need to save for retirement.[1] Don't let that be you!

Happy retirees are typically better budgeters than unhappy ones. They spend more time with their financial planners. They are more comfortable with the level of planning they've done. My survey shows that 79 percent of the happy group is comfortable

Illustration 2.1   Happy Retirees' Levels of Satisfaction with Retirement Planning

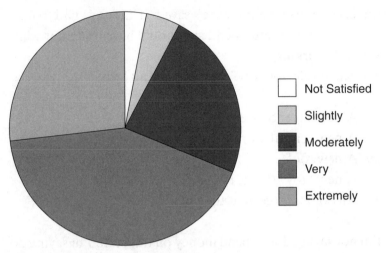

As you can see, the majority of happy retirees are either very happy or extremely happy with the planning they have done.

Illustration 2.2   Unhappy Retirees' Levels of Satisfaction with Retirement Planning

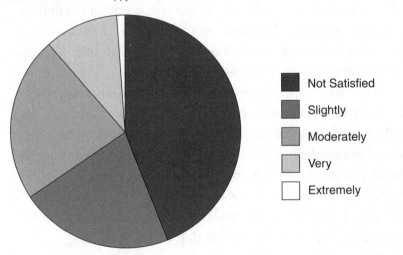

Compare this to the unhappy camp, where almost half of retirees are not satisfied at all.

with the amount of time they've spent planning for their future. Conversely, 87 percent of the unhappy group feels they haven't done enough to plan.

I recently met with a lovely woman named Becky Fallon. She had taken a really expensive riverboat cruise through Europe— from Germany to Amsterdam. It cost her $20,000. She hated herself for it because she knew it was poor planning for the future.

Unhappy retirees rob the budget now and pay for it later. Happy retirees balance the budget now and it pays off later.

Make Sure Your Rich Ratio Is Over 1

This is something I created for the many individuals and families I've worked with over the years, to give them an easy way to understand their money. The Rich Ratio is simply the amount of money you have *in relation* to the amount of money you need. If you have the ability to generate $10,000 a month and you only need $5,000, you're rich! By that same logic, if you have the ability to generate $1 billion a month, but you need $2 billion, you're poor.

Happy retirees honor the rich ratio. Any ratio over 1 is fantastic. Any ratio below that, well—let's just say you have some work to do.

Here's how to find your Rich Ratio. Take the monthly income you will have coming in (social security + pension + any other income streams), including what your nest egg should produce, and divide it by what you expect to spend each month to live the retirement you want:

$$\frac{\text{Have}}{\text{Need}} = \text{Rich Ratio}$$

Example: Jennie has a passion for travel and will need $10,000 per month to support her wanderlust lifestyle in retirement. She has a small pension from her days in the advertising business

($1,000/month) plus social security at age 62 of $1,800/month. She has saved $1,000,000 in her 401(k).

Jennie's Have = $1,000 (pension) + $1,800 (social security) + $4,100 [5% of her 401(k) on a monthly basis] = $6,900

Jennie's Need = $10,000

Jennie's Rich Ratio = $6,900/$10,000 = 0.69

Considering her Rich Ratio is below 1, I would not consider Jennie "rich" at all.

Now let's take a look at Christopher. He needs just $3,500 to live the good life, in part because his house is paid off. Chris also has a small pension ($1,200/month). He will receive social security of $1,800 and has $400,000 in his 401(k).

Christopher's "Have" part of the equation:

Christopher's Have = $1,200 (pension) + $1,800 (social security) + $1,650 [5% of his 401(k) on a monthly basis] = $4,650

Christopher's Need = $3,500

Christopher's Rich Ratio = $4,650/$3,500 = 1.32

Chris's Have is a lot less than Jennie's—but so is his Need, resulting in a 1.32 Rich Ratio, which is beautiful. Even though Christopher has a smaller net worth (and less in retirement savings), he's much richer than Jennie is. Chris is headed for happiness; unfortunately, Jennie is not.

Check Your Pessimism at the Door

When people talk about today's retirement landscape, the message is one of gloom and doom. No one believes he or she will actually be able to retire early. Remember Nick and Katie Benjamin from Chapter 1? Even they had a hard time believing it—and they've been doing everything right.

It goes without saying that we live in an uncertain world. Between 2000 and 2013, the S&P 500 dropped nearly 50 percent on two separate occasions; at one point the NASDAQ dropped 80 percent! In our lifetime we have witnessed real estate plummet by a third in value. Today's 30- and 40-year-olds have either grown up with parents who were burned by the stock market or they've been burned themselves. Many people continue to suffer, still reeling from the financial crisis, the dot-com bubble, and the housing crash.

Until the day she passed away at 107 years old, my Great Aunt Willy V. Ray wouldn't walk past a penny without picking it up. She'd only shop when there was a senior citizen discount. She had plenty of money, but her Depression mentality superseded it. She was a Great Depression baby. What I see today are Great Recession babies: men and women who think about retirement with a great deal of pessimism and fear.

Of course people are scared! There's an explosion in the Middle East every other weekend, tsunamis keep hitting nuclear reactors, and the recent financial crisis drags on and on.

To make matters worse, these things are happening in real time, on 24-hour news networks. Chemical plant fires, school shootings, marathon bombings, murder trials—we watch it all on YouTube or see it in our Facebook feeds. There's no three-day delay to get news from overseas: it's in our face, practically all the time.

No wonder so many people's attitude is: "I don't know if I'll ever be able to retire."

I say: throw out the pessimism! It's not doing you any favors. Can you really retire sooner than you think? Yes. I've seen it happen for hundreds of people. **Fear is paralysis: let it dominate you,**

and nothing seems possible. But if you start taking proactive and preemptive measures today and focus on happiness in retirement, you'll be amazed at what you can do.

Eight Ways to Avoid an Unhappy Retirement

Let's recap eight things you can do to sidestep the unhappy bin:

- **Ditch the BMW and stick to the Asian brands.** The ultimate driving machine is a shiny new money sump—get a car that gives you *comfort* and *cushion* instead.
- **You don't need a second career as a stock trader.** Keep your day job! Not really—you're retired, remember? Avoid changing your investment approach on a whim, and understand the dangers of chasing "hot" investment themes.
- **Give your money a purpose.** Find a cause you are passionate about and contribute either money or time.
- **Don't move, and don't renovate.** They're both too costly—you don't want to start out your retirement in the red.
- **Make big-ticket purchases *before* you retire.** Take care of big purchases one to three years prior to your retirement date, including (but not limited to) new boats, cars, and RVs, expensive artwork, or a pricey vacation.
- **Plan and budget for your retirement.** Happy retirees spend at least five hours a year planning for retirement. You should, too.
- **Make sure your Rich Ratio is over 1.** It's not how much money you have that matters; it's how much you have *in relation* to how much you spend.
- **Check your pessimism at the door.** Pessimism can be costly, and fear is almost always financially devastating. Don't let pessimism lock you out of a stock market and economy that, despite the road bumps, will flourish over time.

CHAPTER 3

Can I Really Retire Sooner Than I Think?

I live in Atlanta—home of the 1996 Summer Olympics and headquarters of Coca-Cola, Home Depot, the Atlanta Braves, and one of the largest airports in the world. It's a city of roughly 6 million people, and it makes the list of the top 10 worst cities for traffic.

One big beltline draws a 64-mile circle around the city—Buckhead, midtown, downtown, and hundreds of "in town" neighborhoods. The majority of the population lives outside the perimeter (OTP) and must commute to inside the perimeter (ITP) each morning.

This is where the traffic nightmare comes to life.

My office is only 12 miles from my home, but it routinely takes anywhere from 25 minutes to an hour to get there. While on the road I see car after car of zombie-eyed individuals making the trek, battling urban sprawl. Every day I get the sense there are millions of hamsters on this wheel—home to work to home to work and then back to home and work again.

The shame is that so many of these working Americans can't see the light at the end of the tunnel. They can't visualize the promise of what was once a traditional retirement. It has been replaced by a sense that the hamster wheel spins for eternity, day in, day out.

It's the same in other cities. Whether it's a carpool in San Francisco or a subway ride in New York City, this sense of a never-ending cycle, of running in place, is destroying the hope of one day retiring like grandma and grandpa did—with a decent monthly pension, a "safe and sound" social security payment, and a nice chunk of savings.

These commuters, for whom the hamster wheel spins, are wondering if they'll ever be able to retire. They're 30, 40, 50 years old, teeming with envy for that nice couple down the street who retired at 56 and now spends every summer at the beach or in the mountains. We all know people like this, and we think: Can that ever be me?

Sure it can. In this chapter, I'll show you how.

But know this: whether you're retiring today or 20 years from today, the economic climate has changed drastically over the last few decades. The sooner you understand how and why, the sooner you can adapt.

How Not to Be Another Scary Statistic

Our parents and grandparents didn't have to worry about retirement: they had a juicy pension waiting for them the moment they left the cubicle where they'd been slaving away for the last 40 years. I probably don't have to tell you times are different now.

In a 2012 article for the investment site *The Motley Fool*, John Reeves points out some scary facts about retirement savings in America.[1] He sources a study from the Employee Benefit Research Institute (EBRI) in which only 42 percent of private sector workers between the ages of 25 and 64 had *any* pension coverage in their current job. And anyone under the age of 50 who still does have a pension program in place will most likely find it far less lucrative than the plans of 30 years ago.

Only 14 percent of American workers reported being "very confident" that they would have enough money to live comfortably in retirement. Only 16 percent of American workers claimed to feel "very confident" about their investments growing in value. Another EBRI study from 2013 revealed:[2]

- 43 percent of all workers think they need to accumulate between $250,000 and $999,999 by the time they retire to live comfortably in retirement.
- 21 percent feel they need between $250,000 and $499,999.

Do these expectations mirror the realities? Not according to the study.

- 57 percent of workers reported that they and/or their spouse had less than $25,000 in total savings and investments (excluding their home and defined benefit plans). This includes 28 percent who had less than $1,000 (up from 20 percent in 2009).

Sound bad? The EBRI study found that nearly half of workers age 45 and older have not even *tried* to calculate how much money they will need to have saved by the time they retire if they want to live comfortably during that retirement.

Planning to let social security carry you into the good life during retirement? Think again. Reeves tells us that for a low earner retiring at 62, social security only replaces 40 percent of preretirement earnings.

Alarmingly, Reeves points out that nearly 75 percent of retirees have not saved enough and would save more if they could do it all over again. It seems like having the ability to find enough financial freedom for retirement at any age would be a modern miracle, right?

Actually, it's not a miracle. But it *does* require making the right choices and persevering, even when times are tough. It means refusing to become another statistic and being proactive with your money instead. I've been privileged to work with hundreds of people whom you might think of as "that rich couple down the street"—who, by the way, probably have less money than you think. They just know what to do with it!

The happy retirees I work with aren't scared by the statistics. They know they're living in trying times, but they also know there are plenty of things under their control—like how much they save, how much they spend, and how they define their life's purpose. They have the five money secrets at the heart of their financial philosophy, and thanks to those secrets, they've established comfort and cushion for themselves. Most important: **they're living happy lives.**

Here's one fascinating finding from my survey: **the people who are happy with their money retire earlier than those who aren't.** The people who are unhappy? Many of them are still working. I get dozens and dozens of phone calls on my radio show from people who are 66, 68, even 70 years old—and they're still punching a time clock. The other day I had a caller on my radio show who was 82 years old and still working!

I don't want you to be one of them. I want you to be able to retire at 62, 60, 55—maybe even 50. And I'm betting you want the same. You don't have to be rich. You just have to sit up and pay attention. If you want to get from point A to B, you have to be ready to fill the gap.

Adopt My Fill the Gap Strategy

The fill the gap strategy (FTG) is at the core of the work I do. But before I explain what it is, let's cover some basics about money and investing.

You can make money in two ways. The first is through appreciation. As an example, I buy a stock at $10, it appreciates over 10 years to $20. I double my money in 10 years—great. The second is through income. I can buy a stock at $10 that pays me a dividend of $1 a year, and I can reinvest that dividend and, 10 years later, I'm at $20 as well.

Both work. Both appreciation and income got me to $20. What my firm does is tell retirees: "We're going to get you a 4 percent yield on your investment." That's just a cash flow. Dividends, interest—all the things that come regularly from owning a dividend specific ETF (exchange traded fund), or Johnson & Johnson stock. Or a pipeline company. Or a bond. With just that part of the equation, you can get to a 3.5, 4, or 4.5 percent yield (alone), which is just the actual cash flow percentage that is paid out to you (or added to your account).

The other part of the equation is growth. How much in overall growth (also known as appreciation) should you expect over time? That part is less predictable, and will rely to some extent on how well the stock market and economy fare in any given year. In a year like 2013 when the U.S. stock market was up more than 30 percent, the growth part of your overall equation (perhaps half of your overall investments) should be up a similar amount, ultimately adding 10 or 15 percent in growth to the overall pie.

However, years like 2013 in the stock market are a somewhat rare occurrence—and not the kind of return you should come to expect or count on. So, on average, I am aiming to gain an additional 2 to 4 percent a year from this part of the equation.

Ultimately, we're trying to get to 6.5 to 7.5 percent a year when you combine those two numbers. Remember, this is with a balanced portfolio of stocks, bonds, and other income-producing investments.

Considering everything we hear about the less-than-stellar rate of return the stock market has shown over the last 12 to 13 years, you may think these numbers sound unrealistic. Not so. Starting from 1926, long-term S&P 500 averages still come in at slightly north of 9 percent per annum. Think of everything that's happened in the world during that span—the Great Depression, multiple wars, assassinations, terror attacks, natural disasters, and the recent Great Recession. Despite all that, the market still averaged a higher return than what we're attempting to get for the people we serve. Feeling optimistic? Good. You should be.

When people are in their twenties, they think, "I don't need dividends, I don't need interest. I just want to buy stocks like Google and watch them go up." That's normal, and smart at that age. You have time to wait and room to maneuver. But as people get older, the strategy changes, and they naturally become more risk-averse. Think of it as a side effect of aging.

The fear most people have about retirement is, "Will I run out of money?" They say, "Wes, I want to get some income, and I don't want my money to run out. Can you do that for me?" They're all trying to fill the gap.

Can I help? Absolutely. It's my job to help them fill the gap (FTG) to ensure their retirement income never runs out.

How do I do it? **By structuring their nest egg to generate enough steady income to fill the gap.** That way they're only eating what's in the fridge. And they never (or rarely) have to dip into the freezer and thaw out their principal.

Here are some initial steps to get your FTG planning underway:

1. **Figure out your income.** It's simple: First, add up all of your guaranteed income streams (pension 1 + pension 2 + social security 1 + social security 2, etc.). This number is your steady monthly stream: it won't change much and is in little danger of fluctuation. Let's say that number is $3,500 a month (after taxes) for you. This is your "take-home income."*

2. **Now, figure out what your monthly spending need is.** An Excel spreadsheet will work, Quicken will work, or just use a good old-fashioned pencil and paper. We have also put one on our website you can use free at http://yourwealth.com/resources-5/retirement -calculator.html. Let's say your monthly expenditures come out to $5,000 a month.

3. **Find your gap.** Subtract your steady income sources from your spending need. $5,000 − $3,500 = a gap of $1,500 a month. That's the perpetual gap you will need to fill—and also an amount that will need to be adjusted higher over time due to inflation.

*You'll want to make sure you perform this exercise with all after-tax dollars. Your pretax income is important, but this exercise looks at "take-home pay" and what you need to spend. And when we spend money, we are spending after-tax dollars. You know your income, you know what you need to spend; now you just need your overall effective tax rate.

Your effective tax rate is an important number to forecast. Bankrate.com has a "1040 Tax Calculator" that will help you get a relatively accurate idea of how much you are paying in taxes today—and what your tax rate will look like in the future as your income drops in retirement. Apply this tax rate to your pretax income to find your take-home income. So if your pre-tax income is

$6,000 a month, you will enter $72,000 annual income. The calculator will show you an overall blended tax rate (if married filing jointly) of about 12 percent in federal taxes. If you are still working and have earned income, understand that you still have to count another 7.65 percent for FICA (social security tax) and Medicare taxes, plus whatever your state income tax is (in Georgia, it's another 6 percent). In California state income tax can fall anywhere from 1 percent to over 12 percent, depending on your income level.

Looks easy, right? Honestly, if your money is being invested the way it should be, it is. *Retirees in the happy group make money work for them, not the other way around.* Let it slowly and steadily grow over time, enjoy the additional income it produces on a monthly or annual basis, and have a blast during retirement. Piece of cake.

Your Financial Situation Is Unique—but Finding the Right Game Plan Will Be Easier than You Think

"But my situation is unique, Wes," you say. "I'm not like those other people. I've got debts and obligations and a big fat mortgage. There's no way I'll ever be able to retire early—I'll never be one of the lucky ones."

Sure, your financial situation is unique, but so is everyone else's. Each weekend, the *Money Matters* team and I field dozens of calls from radio listeners who are dealing with everything under the sun. During the week, I work at an investment planning and tax practice firm alongside 10 other financial advisors, CPAs, and Certified Financial Planner professionals whose job is to help people, no matter what they're dealing with. Every day we respond to a never-ending combination of new financial situations and problems—and we still find ways to help.

Here are just a few of the variations we see:

- Difference in age between spouses
- Married, not married, widowed, and divorced
- Pension versus no pension
- The amount of social security
- The amount of savings
- The number of years until retirement
- The amount of risk and volatility you're willing to take
- Fear of stocks, or love of stocks
- Love of bonds, or fear of bonds
- Business backgrounds
- Medical backgrounds
- Financial discipline
- Addicted to spending, or addicted to saving
- Kids versus no kids
- Grandkids versus no grandkids
- Healthy versus not healthy
- Great healthcare insurance coverage versus minimal healthcare coverage
- Employee versus business owner
- Great retirement plan at work versus absolutely no retirement benefits at work

The list goes on and on. But we've never been thrown by any of these variables. We're still able to help every person who comes through that door.

Why am I telling you this? To assure you that happiness is possible for you, too. Every person has a unique combination of variables, but if you adopt the strategies in this book, you may still be able to retire happy and—with sound planning and hard work—earlier than you thought.

If You Want to Retire Early, Ditch the VIP Mentality

I'll let you in on a secret: I've noticed a distinct difference between the happy retirees I work with today and the people I worked with during my time as vice president of investments at a very well-known Wall Street investment firm. (Without naming names, let's call the firm a global financial juggernaut.) Interestingly, many clients of the firm had a "VIP mentally." They yearned for celebrity treatment. They had money, but many of them weren't at peace with it.

This is different for the families I work with today at my fee-only RIA (registered investment advisor) firm. They are just as wealthy but don't demand extra special treatment. They're more like the inconspicuous millionaires Thomas J. Stanley talks about in *The Millionaire Next Door.* They live in the suburbs of Atlanta, where the houses are between $200,000 and $500,000; they don't live in Buckhead where the houses are $800,000 to $3 million. Think back to Nick and Katie Benjamin and how they took this similar track in order to build an early course toward financial freedom.

For these people, financial planning is less about being a millionaire, or what Stanley would call a PAW (Prodigious Accumulator of Wealth). They march to a different tune, a tune that says, "I've got enough money to be pretty damn comfortable and do what I want to do."

If a happy retiree wants to play golf every day, she can. She doesn't necessarily belong to an ultra-high-end country club that costs $100,000 to join, but she does belong to the Affinity Group of Golf, where she pays a really low monthly fee that allows her to play more than 15 courses across the state of Georgia. Sure, they aren't private clubs with golden mermaids spouting rose-scented water, but they offer a solid consortium of well-maintained courses.

Needless to say, these non-VIP happy retirees really started to catch my eye. Their money provided them with a vehicle to drive toward the things they really wanted to do. As individuals or couples left my office, I'd notice they seemed satisfied with their positions in life. By and large they were having the time of their lives. Here are some examples:

- Marc and Candice love their RV and have hit about half of the states in the United States—they plan on RVing through the rest—including Alaska and Hawaii.
- Emily and Henry love to travel, but have never been to Asia—they are planning a trip there this year.
- Susan and Peter love to watch their granddaughter Brianna, who is in second grade. Brianna's dad and mom both work, but fortunately for the entire family, Susan and Peter are ultra-active grandparents.
- Barney and Dotty are in their early to midsixties and are athletically active. They make it a point each and every day to either go for a walk, take a bike ride, play a round of golf, or play tennis.

All in all, these retirees are simply a much happier group, maybe because they're happier living "in the middle." That doesn't mean they skimp on luxuries—after all, Barney and Dotty go to a nice steak house at least once a week and Emily and Henry love Korean BBQ—but it does mean they know how to put those luxuries in perspective. They're also not interested in "keeping up with the Joneses," because they understand the **plateau effect: after a certain degree of wealth, happiness comes in diminishing returns.**

Stop Using Health Insurance Coverage as an Excuse Not to Retire Early!

Now, I know what you're thinking. "All of this 'retire early' talk sounds great, Wes. And so far most of what I'm reading makes sense. But what about the biggest wild card of all? When are you going to talk about healthcare?"

First, let's clarify our terms: for our purposes, when we talk about healthcare, we're actually talking about *health insurance*. If I retire at 58, or 63, Medicare at age 65 is a long way off. I can't tell you how many clients and radio listeners have come to me and said, "Look, Wes—I'd love to retire early. But I just can't give up the health insurance I get through work."

To which I say: Wake up and smell the new world! The landscape of health insurance for "early retirees" has completely changed with the Affordable Care Act (aka "Obamacare"). It's a game changer, in many ways.

Historically, health insurance has been a major obstacle in the path of early retirement. Traditionally Americans have had to wait until age 65 to receive Medicare. Individuals retiring before that age had to use some sort of stopgap or other coverage option. That included staying under a spouse's health insurance plan, paying for COBRA (a government form of health insurance that only allows for 18 months of coverage and, in some cases, up to 36 months), or going to the private market and buying a policy. In the past, early retirees with no employee-sponsored or legacy-sponsored plan allowing them to maintain coverage until 65 were in serious trouble.

But today, that's old news. As of January 1, 2014, that era is officially behind us with the new implementation of the Affordable Care Act (ACA). Whether you like it *politically* or not, the Affordable Care Act has changed the landscape of retirement planning—especially for people who want to retire early.

To be clear: I'm not here to talk about the politics behind the Affordable Care Act. ACA has been one of the most polarizing political debates that our country has had in a generation. We all know that healthcare costs in America have been rising at an alarming pace—and we also know that demographically, an enormous segment of our population is graying and putting increasing pressure on America's healthcare system.

Healthcare costs in the United States are not my specialty—and it remains to be seen how the ACA will impact the system as a whole. Will it dramatically decrease the cost of healthcare in America over time? Will it solve all of our healthcare problems and woes? I don't know. But I do know there's seldom a silver bullet policy out of Washington that fixes everything the first time. I imagine that we will see several future iterations of the current law.

That said, the new law in its current form will be here for at least a few more years—maybe more. In the meantime, the people who benefit the most from the new model are the very people I'm determined to help: American men and women who want to retire early.

Politics aside, here are the facts: the ACA might help you retire sooner than you think. And if that's true, why not take advantage of it while you can?

Bottom line: One thing stopping Americans retiring pre–age 65 has been the unpredictability of being able to get health insurance coverage, due to any number of either minor or major medical conditions making the cost or ability to buy a private plan inaccessible. Now, regardless of your medical condition, you are able to go to either your state's healthcare exchange or the national exchange (by visiting healthcare.gov) and buy a policy. It may not be the most cost-effective policy, or the best possible coverage on the planet—but it is nonetheless coverage that will protect you from going bankrupt over a significant medical event. And it will bridge the gap until Medicare kicks in at age 65.

For a more detailed explanation of the new Affordable Care Act, visit my website* where you'll find special bonus material, including a full explanation of the new American healthcare system and real-life examples of how happy retirees have used the new laws to their full advantage—and tips on how you can do the same. (Visit www.yourwealth.com and use the search word "ACA" to find the bonus material.)

Keep the Plateau Effect in Mind

Remember the "plateau effect," where after a certain level of wealth is achieved, people experience a diminishing return of happiness? The plateau effect doesn't just show up in regard to income, as we saw in the Preface. The exact same thing happens with spending: happiness tapers off after a certain point.

- **Average spending** from the unhappy group of retirees jumps 25 percent to reach the next level (the slightly happy retirees). But then spending levels begin to level out and rise at a much slower pace, eventually becoming remarkably similar.
- **Median spending** jumps by 60 percent from the unhappiest retirees to the next level of retiree. But then, once we're into the happy retiree categories, it levels off *significantly*.

You might expect spending levels to shoot way up as happiness levels rise, but look at the graphs from my proprietary money and happiness survey in Illustration 3.1. The results might surprise you.

Illustration 3.1   Happiness by Spending Level (Mean)

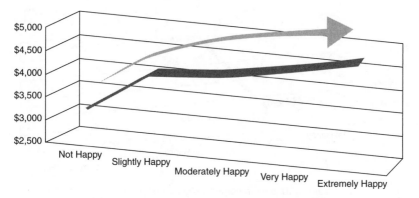

As you can see from the graph, the plateau effect is on full display here. After a certain point, spending more does little to increase happiness levels.

Look at the mean (or average) data for each group. From the not happy to slightly happy group, spending jumps a noticeable 25 percent. But between the next four gradations of happy— slightly, moderately, very, extremely—spending only jumps 2 percent, 5 percent, and 6 percent respectively. Yes, the "average level of spending per month" rises, but not significantly. Slightly happy retirees spend $4,000 a month on average, while very happy retirees spend not much more.

What kind of income would it take to be able to spend $4,000 to $4,100 a month? A family would have to generate about $58,800 in pretax income to net $50,000 ($4,100 × 12 months = $49,200, rounded to $50,000).

Netting $50,000 at a 15 percent overall tax rate would require a family to have a pretax income of $58,822. Thus, up to a certain point, more spending means more happiness, but once a family reaches a median level of around $50,000 a year, there's a decreasing amount of additional happiness with each dollar spent.

The plateau effect strikes again, serving as further evidence that more income and more spending only lead to more happiness *up to a point*. That point is very attainable to most Americans. (Note: This means you!)

Illustration 3.2   Happiness by Liquid Net Worth (Median)

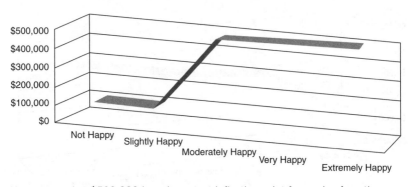

You can see that $500,000 is an important inflection point for moving from the unhappy group to the happy group, but after that, not much changes.

What about liquid net worth? Is there a plateau effect with your stocks, bonds, mutual funds, and cash? Take a look at Illustration 3.2.

The unhappy and slightly happy retirees have a liquid net worth slightly north of $100,000. If you move up the graph to the moderately happy retirees, you'll see liquid net worth jumps all the way to $500,000. Looking at the data in this way shows that $500,000 in liquid net worth is an important inflection point.

Want to Retire Early?
Be Like the Happy Retirees

Marc and Carol Hobbs are a prototypical happy retiree family. They're one of those couples who seem to be having fun all the time. Hard to find a day of the week Marc isn't playing golf, and Carol's the same way—always relaxed, always headed somewhere to play tennis or help with the grandkids. And that's when they're not vacationing in exotic sunny locales.

How do they accomplish this lifestyle without being "super rich"? Marc and Carol live their lives by the five money secrets—and they were able to retire at 61 and 58, respectively.

Or take James and Wendy Camp. The Camps love working part-time, hiking Stone Mountain weekly, cycling for exercise, and going on cycling tours with large groups—Tuscany, Colorado, Washington State, you name it. They stay very fit, and Wendy retired early (at 62) to enjoy her many pursuits. If you think this is out of range for you, you're wrong.

They say it's never a good idea to compare yourself to others, but I disagree. If you see someone standing where you want to be standing, study that person! Figure out how he or she got there and what you need to do or change to arrive at the same place. As you read, I want you to start comparing yourself to the happy retirees in these pages. Take a look at the ways they've made the right choices financially—and figure out how you can do the same.

I've done the research for you. Those 1,350 retirees I surveyed? They're featured in this book, spilling their secrets—about their core pursuits, lack of a mortgage, multiple income sources, savings, and the ways they became income investors.

Can you really retire sooner than you think? Sure you can. In this book, you'll learn from the best.

Next on the Docket: Five Money Secrets

Purpose, Savings, Mortgage, Income, and Income Investing: these five money secrets are at the core of any happy retirement. In the chapters that follow, we'll discuss each of these in greater depth.

Purpose

Money Secret #1: Determine What You Want
and Need Your Retirement Money For

What do you want to do with your life when you retire? Happy retirees all have passions and at least three *core pursuits* they yearn to accomplish. In Chapter 4 we'll see that core pursuits are the key drivers of the entire happy retiree journey.

Savings

Money Secret #2: Figure Out How Much Money You Need to Save Before You Retire

For every $240,000 you have saved for retirement, you can expect to have $1,000 a month at your disposal, provided you don't retire before you hit your sixties. If you have more than $240,000, great. I like working with multiples of that number: $480,000, $720,000, $960,000, $1,200,000, $1,440,000, and so on. In Chapter 5 we'll talk about how to translate these numbers into happiness.

Mortgage

Money Secret #3: Pay Off Your Mortgage in as Little as Five Years

Sooner or later, every homeowner asks the simple question, "Should I pay off my mortgage?" and immediately is bombarded with a variety of complicated, hedged responses. Here is the simplest possible answer: Yes. If you are anywhere near retirement and can afford to pay off your mortgage, you should. I'll dedicate all of Chapter 6 to showing you how to make it happen.

Income

Money Secret #4: Develop an Income Stream from Three or Four Sources, Not Just One

We get used to receiving a W-2 paycheck or paying ourselves (as business owners) while we're in our yeoman working years—one big paycheck to rule them all. This mentality has to change as we head into retirement, if not before. We have to go from one *big* income stream to a bunch of little ones. In Chapter 7, we'll discuss the following income sources and more:

- Part-time work
- Part-time consulting
- Rental income
- Investment income (various types—Chapter 8 is dedicated to this)
- Social security (if you get it)
- Pension income (if you have it)

Income Investing

Money Secret #5: Become an Income Investor

In Chapter 8, I will submit my very own "bucket" approach, which is going to shift your whole investment paradigm. The bucket approach takes a very complex world of investing and simplifies it tremendously by helping you visualize your investments as money dropped into one of four easy-to-understand buckets.

This bucket diagram that I will walk you through is at the very heart of my "be happy in retirement" financial philosophy. It's something that really resonates with our radio listeners and the families we work with direclty. I believe in trying to generate steady levels of income through dividends, interest, and distributions. Those three areas add up to a portfolio yield—something predictable in an otherwise unpredictable market.

Sound good to you? Read on.

PART TWO

The 5 Money Secrets of Happy Retirees

CHAPTER 4

Secret #1

Determine What You Want and Need Your Retirement Money For

Marilyn Noble is 62 years old and married to Jerry, who is 66. The couple has one grown daughter. When Marilyn comes into my office, she is lively and full of vigor. She moves at 90 miles an hour and has no intention of slowing down after she retires. For Marilyn and Jerry Noble, life is just starting to get good.

Marilyn would never describe herself as wealthy. She isn't CEO of a Fortune 500 Company or heiress to a hotel empire. Marilyn is an eleventh grade AP language and composition teacher, and she recently earned a 25-year length of service number in the State of Georgia's Teacher Retirement System (TRS). She's not rich in a traditional sense. Her liquid net worth is well south of $1 million.

On one of her more recent office visits, Marilyn wanted to know if she could retire this year or if she would need to wait. I had an answer for her—and it's not the answer she was expecting.

This chapter is all about the importance of *purpose*—figuring out what you want and need your retirement money *for*. I want to start by telling you about the life and finances of Marilyn Noble. I've known Marilyn for years, and "purpose" might as well be her middle name.

Marilyn is going to have a small but meaningful pension from the Georgia TRS—about $2,800 a month. She will also be able to receive social security income, but the amount is drastically reduced for her. This is because the TRS and teachers struck a deal that raised future pensions in exchange for lowering future social security payments. So even at 65, her social security will only be $400 a month.

Jerry, like many other sixty-somethings in America, has basically worked for one employer his entire life. His social security is going to be higher, at $1,950 a month. After all these years he has a tiny pension of $185 a month. As you can see, none of these are big numbers.

Jerry's 401(k) is $60,000. All of Marilyn's retirement accounts, her teacher's 403(b) plan, add up to $630,000. Their combined liquid retirement assets are $690,000.

I analyze these numbers, incorporating all the various income streams she has available to her now, and it comes to $4,935 a month. Marilyn says to me, "I need more than that. I need $6,500 a month." If we incorporate taxes into the equation, Marilyn will actually need approximately $7,500 a month to net down to $6,500 in spending.

I ask her why she needs $6,500 a month, and she says it's the amount that will allow her to maintain two small houses, travel twice a year, maintain her Jet Skis, pay entrance dues for her music competitions, keep the lights on, etc. In other words, she feels she needs $6,500 a month to live the life she wants to live.

I take $7,500 as the pretax need and subtract the guaranteed streams of pretax income—the $4,935. She needs a $2,565 boost per month in order to live the life she wants to live. How's she going to get that?

This is why she hired me. It's my job to help Marilyn *fill the gap* (FTG) in her income.

And here's how I do it.

Marilyn is going to take her $690,000, and she's going to be an income investor. She's going to pull approximately 4.5 percent of that number: $31,050 a year. Divide that by 12. That's about $2,600 a month. That fixes the deficit. Marilyn wins.

She now has $4,935 a month, plus $2,600. All of a sudden her gross income is right near the $7,500 she needs to net the $6,500 a month—a monthly amount that should be sustainable for the remainder of her life (and Jerry's, too).

It's fantastic that Marilyn was able to reach the amount of money she needed, but it is not necessarily coincidental. Like the Benjamins, the Nobles have planned well. We were able to add up Marilyn's assets, figure out what they could produce for her, and then tailor her budget to that number.

The next component is that Marilyn's house is worth $450,000, on which she owes $100,000. She's going to sell the house for $450,000, pay off the mortgage, and end up with $350,000.

Here's where things start to get fun. Marilyn takes the $350,000 and buys two properties. First she gets a very nice small condo/townhouse a little bit outside of Atlanta for $200,000. She pays for it in cash. No mortgage. Depending on where you live, you might be thinking, "Um, Wes? What kind of dump can she get for $200,000?" But in Atlanta that's very realistic—Marilyn finds an awesome place.

Marilyn also has a little plot of land on the remote Lake Fontana in North Carolina. She and Jerry are going to take that $150,000 and build a 1,800-square-foot cabin on that lot as their second property. Romantic? You'll have to ask them. That's out of my jurisdiction.

Marilyn just aced money secret #3: she no longer has a mortgage. Pop the no-mortgage champagne—the sweetest vintage in town.

Does Marilyn have to worry about all those "other" expenses like property taxes, homeowner's insurance, condo assessments, maintenance fees, etc.? Yes, but don't fret. All that was already accounted for in the $6,500-a-month budget.

What's so great about Marilyn's plan is that she has two different places. She can go back and forth. The reason she still wants to have a place in Atlanta is because she loves art, music, and the culture of Atlanta. She goes to the High Museum, the Alliance Theatre, and is a dedicated patron of Georgia Shakespeare. And she absolutely loves the symphony. She gets symphony tickets with her friends the Millers, and together they go six or eight times a year. Marilyn and Jerry have a whole list of cool cultural stuff they do. She also wants to maintain the condo in Atlanta because her doctors and dentists are here.

But the real reason I'm telling you the story of Marilyn Noble is because she's an absolute all-star when it comes to money secret #1: **know what your retirement money is for—and use the hell out of it.**

Marilyn is one of my favorite happy retirees because her core pursuits are the stuff of legend. She proudly celebrates her Scottish roots by playing in a Scottish band. Jerry is a bagpiper, and Marilyn is a flourishing tenor drummer. Once a year in Atlanta her band hosts the Stone Mountain Highland Games—a Highland festival where people wear Scottish kilts and eat Scottish food. Her band competes four times a year. Marilyn told me she has too much to do to go to work!

Marilyn's 35-year-old daughter lives in rural Georgia and recently set up something called the Backyard Market. It's a local food market, selling local clothes, local art, wooden bowls—the whole nine yards. Marilyn is going to help her daughter get her new business off the ground. Can you imagine a more rewarding way to bond with your adult child?

Marilyn is Catholic. She and Jerry go to Mass every Sunday in Atlanta, and there's a small church near Lake Fontana she attends when she's there. She is also a member of the St. Andrew's Society—another Highlands Association nonprofit. In fact, she does their newsletter every quarter. You could say she's well-rounded.

Marilyn also volunteers. Most happy retirees do. Marilyn serves at the Pregnancy Aid Center, helping pregnant moms and teens manage their financial habits. She travels to Hapeville, Georgia to do this twice a month—and that's on top of her teaching schedule.

In case you couldn't tell, Marilyn is active. She works out, doing circuit training a couple of times a week. She swims at the YMCA. She water skis. She has two used Jet Skis up at Lake Fontana that she'll be using more often once the cabin is built.

Not to be outdone, Jerry works out at the gym four times a week. He loves to learn. He'll soon be taking classes at Georgia State University in downtown Atlanta. He's going to get a degree in music. He plays the guitar, the banjo, and the dulcimer. (Yeah, I don't really know what it is, either. But apparently Jerry can rock out on it.)

Are you starting to wish you could retire *today*? I can't promise that, but I will promise you can do it sooner than you think if you emulate people like the Nobles. They saved money for a purpose, and now they can spend it on their retirement dreams.

This summer Jerry and Marilyn are taking a trip. They'll start in Vancouver, then go over to Victoria, then to a Highlands festival, then Jasper, then Banff, then Calgary, then back to Atlanta. It's going to be their fortieth anniversary trip and their celebration of retirement—now that I gave them the green light to retire.

Despite all this, Marilyn recently confessed something to me. "You know what, Wes?" she said. "I might want to work part-time. There are a couple of things I'd love to do, just for fun, and walk home at the end of the night and not have to worry about it." I wasn't surprised at all. Marilyn is the type of person who engages with life wherever she is. Of course she'd want to find a fun job—and add another income stream to boot.

Remember how Katie Benjamin plans to work in real estate and teach spin classes after she's retired? I hope you're starting to see a pattern. The physical activity, the part-time jobs, the staying engaged with friends and colleagues—any way you slice it, the retirees in the happy group know what they're doing.

Marilyn is the ultimate happy retiree. She and Jerry display every one of the five money secrets you'll learn in this book. She's got a little bit of income from a lot of places. We found a way to make sure she gets 4 to 5 percent from her savings and use those streams to fill the gap for the rest of her life. She has a ton of core pursuits and passions and no mortgage. She has two fully paid for, very different homes in different environments—one in the country, one in the city.

The day I finished analyzing Marilyn's numbers, she told me she could technically retire in July but that she'd get an extra $70 a month if she waited another year. Do you know what I told her? I told her to retire *today*. I wouldn't let her wait an extra year for $70! She doesn't need it to live the life she wants to live.

Marilyn Noble, at 62, is retiring sooner than she thought.

Marilyn texted Jerry right then and there—from our meeting. I wish I could have been there to see his face when the words "WE CAN RETIRE IN 2014!" appeared on the screen.

Bravo Marilyn. Couldn't happen to a nicer person.

And *you* could be next.

You Get to Choose the Kind of Life You Want to Lead

"But Wes," you say. "I can't just join a Scottish band and expect to be a happy retiree."

Nor should you. What works for Marilyn Noble won't work for you—and vice versa. The trick is to figure out what *you* want, and how your money will fuel the life *you* want to live.

You've worked hard and saved money, but what good is it unless you know how you want to spend it?

This is uncharted territory for the standard retirement planning book. Most will teach you how to make money but stop there. What do you do with it once you have it? Does that part just take care of itself? No, it does not. You have to choose. Part of showing you how to retire early is showing you how to retire happy. **It doesn't happen because of the money you save, but rather with the help of that money.**

Let's do an exercise. Don't worry—it will be relatively quick and painless (I promise you won't sweat). Get out a pen or pencil, and answer the following eight questions right here in this book.

1. How many vacations would you like to take each year?

   _____

2. Where would you like to travel? What places do you want to see? (Could include both exotic locales and local treasures.)

   _____

   _____

3. What are some activities you'd like to get involved in? Activities you'd like to get *more* involved in?

   _____

   _____

4. What have you been putting off or letting slip that you would like to change, starting this year—and especially during your retirement years? Spending more time with friends, reconnecting with old acquaintances, taking a women's trip, taking a guys' trip, enjoying more time with family? Devoting more time to exercising or eating healthier?

    _____

    _____

    _____

5. What does a "perfect day" or even just a "fulfilling day" in retirement look like for you? Sketch out a rough schedule below:

    8 a.m. _____

    10 a.m. _____

    12 noon _____

    2 p.m. _____

    4 p.m. _____

    6 p.m. _____

    8 p.m. _____

    10 p.m. _____

6. Are there sports or activities you're interested in playing or learning? Some ideas: golf, tennis, sailing, ceramics, collage, or photography.

    _____

    _____

7. What communities would you like to be more involved in? Some ideas: your church, neighborhood association, Rotary Club, Kiwanis Club, a local park conservancy, or local Jewish Community Center.

    _____

    _____

8. What are some nonprofits and organizations where you might like to volunteer?

_____

_____

There are no right or wrong answers here—this list will look different for everyone. All I'm trying to do is get you to start being honest about why you want money and what you want to do with it. **Remember: it isn't about the money; it's about the money providing the framework for the life you want to live.**

The sooner you can get clear on that, the sooner you can start working toward your goals.

Core Pursuits: Why You Need Them

Think of a core pursuit as a hobby on steroids. It isn't just something you dabble in; it's something that drives and fulfills you. You don't need a million of them, but you do need at least three. A core pursuit should help define you, bringing into focus the things that matter most. You do it often, and you think about it even more.

My father has always been a man with many core pursuits. In fact, even though he is in a position to retire, he still hasn't pulled the trigger yet. He still isn't ready to give up life as a veterinarian running his own practice, curing all kinds of cats and dogs. (In fact, according to him, I owe a big thank-you to golden retrievers, as their predisposition toward hip dysplasia helped him afford to put me through college. Thanks, Old Yeller.)

But being a vet is just his occupation—it doesn't come close to defining him. My father is a Civil War reenactor and historian. He's a leather-smith, meaning he makes his own bridles and saddles for the Percheron he rides (by the way, if you haven't seen a Percheron, just imagine a slightly smaller version of the

Budweiser Clydesdale). Dad is also an amateur blacksmith, an amateur dressage and steeplechase rider, and a guitar player. He spent two years as a pirate reenactor until discovering he got seasick on ships. He's been, by turn, a furniture maker, trail rider, softball enthusiast, and mountain biker. He's even into fencing, preferring the saber to the épée or foil.

You can see why I grew up with an innate appreciation of core pursuits!

My father's pursuits have never fallen into the traditional categories. He doesn't like to travel, doesn't even believe in playing golf. Yet he's always been the kind of man who could retire on Monday and be even busier on Tuesday because of all his core pursuits. He loves them so much! He has a tremendous sense of all these things burning inside him *in addition* to his job as a veterinarian specializing in orthopedic surgery (which he still loves).

I've always looked to emulate that in my life. If you want to be one of the happiest retirees, you need to do the same. I inherently knew it was going to be a tremendous part of the happiness equation because I had witnessed how my dad's core pursuits have kept him younger than his years. It's one of the fundamentals of retirement happiness; I won't budge an inch on this one. If you want to be happy in retirement, you must have core pursuits!

As we've seen, Marilyn Noble is a great example of a happy retiree who has a strong, exciting set of core pursuits that feed and fulfill her. Now let's take a look at her polar opposite: Arthur McMullen.

Find Pursuits That Excite You—Don't Be Like Mac

Arthur "Mac" McMullen was a guy I used to work for here in Atlanta. He was part of a big utility company and worked there for 32 years. He ended up with a good pension, several million dollars in company stock, and a 401(k) with close to $3 million.

The problem was, Mac was so wrapped up in his career he did little else. As he would put it, he had no core pursuits at all. Even though he was able to retire at a fairly young age—63—he soon found himself battling depression. He had never been depressed in his life, but without work, he lost the only identity and sense of purpose he had ever known.

Was money an issue? No. Mac had plenty of that, and plenty of time to spend it. The problem was that he had no idea what to *do* with all his money and time. It's pretty tough to start playing golf when you're 63 years old!

It's important to understand at an early age that having a core set of things you love to do is part of having optimal health—part of having a healthy balance when it comes to work and family and your own psyche. You can't just work for the dream of having a big pile of money—unless your life's purpose is swimming in a huge pile of money. And if that is the case, I think you might have some other problems. It worked for Scrooge McDuck, but it probably won't work for you.

Money itself doesn't mean anything to us. Why would it? Do the pages of a book mean anything? Of course not. It's the meaning of the words arranged on those pages that makes a book significant. Money works the same way. It only has the meaning we assign to it. Be the master of that money. Make it serve your purpose and help you achieve what you are truly passionate about in your own life.

If you're getting close to retirement and you only have one or two things you like to do outside of work, I have bad news: You're probably going to be unhappy. Don't blame me—it's all in the data. Look at Illustrations 4.1 and 4.2.

What are you waiting for? Go get three to five core pursuits right now! I want you to test out three to five new things in your

Illustration 4.1   Happy Retirees' Number of Core Pursuits

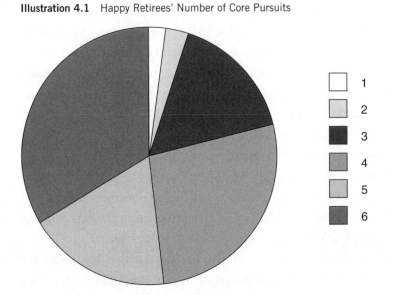

Illustration 4.2   Unhappy Retirees' Number of Core Pursuits

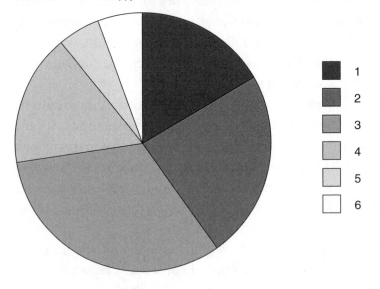

Learn from the happy retirees: have three core pursuits—at the very least! Even better if there are four or five activities you love.

life. If you have zero when you retire, you'll be in bad shape—no matter how much money you have.

Here are three easy ways to ensure you're not moving toward a McMullen retirement:

1. **Get three to five core pursuits.** I don't really care what they are. I grew up with a father who thought golf was a ridiculous pastime, but making horseshoes for his Percheron named Buster so they would be ready for the next Civil War reenactment was okay. So *what* core pursuits you fall in love with doesn't matter—as long as they mean the world to you. Some people live for golf, some Scottish dance, some biking in Tuscany, and some just love making horseshoes.

2. **Rock out.** Music is one of those core pursuits that's mildly undercover. It often gets missed in conversation because it can take on so many forms. But happy retirees love music. Sound a little strange? It did to me, too. But if you listen for it, you'll realize how often music plays a role in these people's lives. It manifests in different ways: The church choir. Teaching piano. Singing in the car like Jerry Maguire. Big concerts, little concerts. Jazz, rock, the symphony. Playing music—in bands, on the piano, or on the guitar at home. And yes, even karaoke. Happy retirees love moving and grooving!

3. **Be active and be social.** After working with so many happy retirees, it is very clear to me that physical activity is an important ingredient in their happiness. Even if you don't love the gym or you hate jogging, some form of exercise is critical. Regular exercise isn't just great for you physically; it's a huge boon mentally as well. Chalk it up to extra endorphins, if you want.

Or maybe it gives you time to think about and work out life's problems in your head. It could even be the fact that so much exercise-related activity is also very social—basketball leagues, softball leagues, water polo teams (a favorite at The Villages in Florida), exercise boot camps, running groups, cycling tour groups, you name it. Keep in mind that being active can serve as a social outlet, too.

Diversifying Your Core Pursuits

The number one core pursuit for happy retirees is volunteering. That's no coincidence. These men and women feel like they are truly accomplishing something, and it gives them an immense sense of satisfaction—even euphoria. The happiest couples and individuals I work with beam from ear to ear when they talk about the charities they support.

The options for volunteering are endless. There are food banks, church volunteer programs, veteran organizations, wounded warrior programs, disabled groups, and alumni associations. Wherever and however you decide to pitch in, it's important to volunteer. If you don't already participate at your kid's school, your church, or a community foundation, go find two to three places where you can give your time, effort, or money. That way you'll never run the risk of being curmudgeonly Mac McMullen.

In addition to volunteering, the next three most popular core pursuits in the happy retiree camp include travel, spending time with grandkids and family, and golf—in that order. But those are far from the only pursuits that show up. It's fascinating to me how diverse the world of retirees is when it comes to core pursuits. When I think of most of the happy men retirees I work with in Atlanta, they want to play golf and tennis and travel. I think that's awesome for them, but you don't need to have those specific activities as your core pursuits to be happy. You just have to have some things you love.

I already told you how Marilyn Noble does Scottish festivals and plays drums in the band, volunteers at the Pregnancy Aid Center, and does the newsletter for the St. Andrews Society. She also water-skis and Jet Skis up at Lake Fontana. Believe it or not, those are just a few of the core pursuits Marilyn enjoys.

I know happy retirees who build ham radios in their basement and sell them on the Internet. Others work part-time. Atlanta is the land of Home Depot, and I can't tell you how many retirees I know who end up working there part-time. Their attitude is: "I used to go there all the time and shop, why not get paid to hang out?" They've taken a core pursuit and turned it into a productive way to enjoy retirement.

Do the Home Depot jobs pay minimum wage? Some of the jobs there are close—but my retirees aren't doing it for the money. They're doing it because they love tools, and plumbing, and HVAC, and lighting! You know those guys who really get a kick out of coming to your house and fixing something broken? That's them! "Oh, your door fell off the cabinet? I know how to fix that. I'll Gorilla Glue it, get a couple of vice grips, let 'er bake overnight, and she'll be good as new."

There's an air of productivity to the Home Depot crowd—a sense of pride in wearing the orange apron, as opposed to the Walmart blue. I actually hear people say "I don't want to be a greeter at Walmart" as a euphemism for wanting to find an interesting core pursuit. It's entered the American vernacular. So, they take off the blue and put on the orange. I'm certainly happy about it, because I need all the help I can get when it comes to home improvement and would be lost at Home Depot if it weren't for all of those orange aprons.

There's also an avid car culture—car shows, weekend car trips. There are wine connoisseurs and foodies. There's the college football crowd, or as I call them, tailgaters! They set up the beer and barbeque every Saturday for three months, possibly longer if the Georgia Bulldogs are ranked in the top 10. In fact, the Bulldogs are even more popular than Atlanta's professional football team, the Atlanta Falcons. My radio station carries college football and doesn't even carry the Falcons. SEC football is king down south.

Church is huge in Atlanta. In fact, because it airs on Sunday morning, my radio show has a large number of people listening as they get ready for, commute to, or commute from church. They tell me, "Wes, I wish I could listen more but the pastor is gonna kill me if I don't get out of my car and go inside." From Lutherans, to Baptists, to Presbyterians, to Catholics, to Jews—people are passionate about church (or synagogue) here in the South.

The point I'm making is that the options are endless. You have so much to choose from. All that I'm asking is for you to look inside yourself, figure out what it is that gets your motor running, and find a way to make that a part of your retirement plan.

Don't Be a Loner: A Vibrant Social Life Leads to Greater Happiness

Have you noticed how the happy retirees have core pursuits that are typically social in nature? The most popular activities of unhappy retirees are reading, hunting, writing, and fishing. There's nothing wrong with any of those, but they are by and large solitary activities. There's a time for solitude—but my survey shows that it rarely leads to happiness.

A core pursuit can be the mere act of being social. I like to go out on Friday nights. Whether it's a date night with my wife or just having dinner with friends, it's important to me. I'm very consistent with it. The sense of being social and communal is very important to my happiness, and whether you know it or not, it's important to yours.

In *The Blue Zones*, author Dan Buettner discusses the propensity for community and its possible effect on lifespan. One of the cities Buettner cites as an example is Loma Linda, California. Located about 60 miles east of Los Angeles, Loma Linda houses roughly 9,000 Seventh-Day Adventists. Without going too much into the religion itself, Adventists place a strong emphasis on communal time—decompressing on the Sabbath, community potluck socials, and volunteering. Is it a coincidence that they have longer life spans than most people in America? Buettner says no, and I would agree.

Another example Buettner uses is the Greek island of Ikaria. Like Loma Linda, this region houses a cluster of residents whose life span far exceeds the world average. While studies have shown the increased health may have to do with drinking a certain type of boiled coffee, Buettner believes it's more about the people they were drinking it with.[1] He observed that the people of Ikaria enjoy their coffee with others, and they let the visit linger in pleasant conversation.

I'm not making the case that longer life is solely a result of the strong sense of community, but it sure seems to play an important role. I don't like using the word *magical*, but there is something about interacting with neighbors that seems to nourish the soul. Maybe it's time to build yourself a front porch and invite some friends over. (Just remember to pay the contractor *before* you retire.)

Connecting with others, even in an impromptu setting, can make for a powerful sense of community. Maybe you run into your neighbors while you're both taking the kids to school or bump into a friend while you're out walking the dog. We can all agree these are pleasant, uplifting moments of connection (unless you're feuding with your neighbor, of course). It turns out we're not alone in this world, and that realization makes for a healthier, happier life.

Exercise Your Right to Be Healthy

Another hugely important area is exercise, as it leads to vitality and health. You didn't buy this book for workout tips, but it's a very important topic. It's also part of why golf is such a popular core pursuit for retirees—it's a bridge to the exercise. It provides retirees with a chance for some fresh air with other people, and a chance to challenge themselves to be better at something. You can exercise the mind and the body. You can compete with yourself. It's a mixture of exercise, community, and self-improvement.

Golf is so popular that some people play it twice a week or more. In these cases, they have my blessing to count it as more than just one core pursuit. It's one activity, but you can do it so much and so religiously that it can carry more weight.

Have you noticed how exercise tends to crop up as a core pursuit for happy retirees? The happiest people who call into my radio show or come into my office tend to be physically active. Dozens of my clients run triathlons. Some run full length, some run mini-triathlons, and some crank it all the way up to Ironman levels. Drive around cities like Atlanta or Denver or Los Angeles, and you'll see bumper stickers that say "26.2" to signify the number of miles in a marathon. Or you'll see "140.6," which is the Ironman length.

Want to try some of the physical activities that the happiest retirees enjoy? Move your body and:

- Walk
- Jog
- Hike
- Bike

- Play tennis
- Do Pilates
- Do yoga
- Golf
- Swim
- Sign up for a charity walk or run (5k, 10k, etc.)
- Take a spinning class
- Join a boot camp
- Join a gym
- Train for a half-marathon/marathon/triathlon
- Do CrossFit
- Try Orangetheory Fitness
- Take a Cardio Barre class

The key here is to be active and try something physical on a regular basis. It will make you feel better, live healthier, and lead to a better life.

I can assure you an overwhelming majority of happy retirees partake in activities such as these. One of the biggest 10k races in the world is the Peachtree Road Race in Atlanta. There is a whole community of people who do it. Tens of thousands of people run it—and that number includes more of my clients than you might think. Would they do it if it didn't make them happy?

It's Not Too Late to Re-Create Yourself by Finding Core Pursuits

If you don't have core pursuits, I want you to get some. If you're 35 or 45, start thinking about whether or not you've struck a healthy balance in your life. Do it now so you already have at least three core pursuits in place by the time you retire.

But even if you're 65, it's not too late. This is the best advice I can give you: Go find the stuff you love. As George Bernard Shaw said, "Life isn't about finding yourself. Life is about creating yourself." I couldn't have said it better myself.

Here's a quick, fun exercise that will get you thinking about how to "re-create" yourself. Still have that pen handy? Great. Spend the next three minutes listing out the 20 wildest things you've always wanted to do. This could be the stuff you've always thought, "That would be crazy! I'll never pull it off." But don't censor yourself; write it all down. As prominent author Neale Donald Walsch says: "Life begins at the end of your comfort zone."

I'll get you started with some ideas: skydiving, scuba diving off the coast of Australia, doing an Ironman triathlon, writing a novel, writing a nonfiction book, starting a league for your favorite sport, becoming a coach, running for public office, selling a painting, starting a company, learning Italian, learning guitar, climbing a mountain, going to India or Russia, going to the Olympics, making a movie, being in a movie, living on an Amish farm for a week—or having lunch with Warren Buffet or Jimmy Buffet.

Feel free to steal any of those if they strike you as something you want to do, but come up with stuff that touches your heart. The sky's the limit. Most important: have fun with it! It isn't every day you get to mold your future into whatever shape you want it to be.

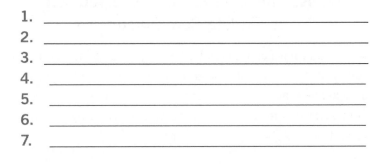

1. _____
2. _____
3. _____
4. _____
5. _____
6. _____
7. _____

8. _____
9. _____
10. _____
11. _____
12. _____
13. _____
14. _____
15. _____
16. _____
17. _____
18. _____
19. _____
20. _____

Now circle the top five you want to do before the age of
_____ (you decide: 60? 70? 85? 100?).

Once you have your top five circled, do the following:

- Search the web and find out what it would take to carry out these crazy ideas.
- Find out where these wildly interesting activities would be located.
- Figure out a price range of the full experience from start to finish.
- Set a start date for at least one of these endeavors before the end of this year.
- Don't listen to anyone who tries to discourage you—they'll probably end up in the unhappy camp.

CHAPTER 5

Secret #2

Figure Out How Much Money You Need to Save Before You Retire

Shel Silverstein's classic children's book *The Giving Tree* describes the relationship between a boy and a tree that loves him. "Every day the boy would come to the tree to eat her apples, swing from her branches, or slide down her trunk . . . and the tree was happy. But as the boy grew older he began to want more from the tree, and the tree gave and gave."[1]

Eventually, the boy exhausts all of the resources and gifts that the tree has to offer—all that remains is a stump.

I want you to imagine this stump when you think about your portfolio.

If you use your portfolio the way the boy used the tree—to climb, to eat its fruit, to sell its timber, and then give nothing in return—your portfolio will resemble that stump of dead wood. A portfolio is a living, breathing entity, and you want to keep it healthy and happy.

In this chapter, I'll show you how to supplement your retirement income with your retirement savings—your nest egg. We're going to figure out the formula for how much money you need to have saved before you retire.

The 1,000-Bucks-a-Month Rule

The first part of the formula is simple: the 1,000-Bucks-a-Month Rule. This is one of my all-time favorites. If there's one rule my radio listeners and happy retirees remember, this would be it.

Simply put, here's how the 1,000-Bucks-a-Month Rule works: **For every 1,000 bucks per month you want to have at your disposal in retirement, you need to have $240,000 saved.**

Consider why $240,000 in the bank equals $1,000 a month:

$240,000 × 5% (withdrawal rate) = $12,000
$12,000 divided by 12 months = $1,000 a month

That's how I like to break it down: in increments of $1,000. And each $1,000:

- Supplements social security income
- Supplements pension income
- Supplements part-time work income
- Supplements any other streams you can manage to establish

Depending on the size of your social security, pension, or part-time work streams, the number of $240,000 multiples you'll need to save will vary. What doesn't vary is the rule itself. The 1,000-Bucks-a-Month Rule is a crucial piece of the jigsaw puzzle. For every $1,000 you want each month in retirement, it is imperative you save $240,000.

"But Wes," you say. "How do we get to 5 percent? That's a pretty significant percentage, isn't it?" Sure it is—especially when there are periods of time (sometimes entire decades) when the stock market itself barely has any gain. But don't worry: I'm not setting you up for unrealistic expectations. The 5 percent withdrawal rate is predicated on the following two key factors:

1. **Income investing.** Income investing tells us there should be a certain amount of "cash flow" produced from your investments—no matter what. If that cash flow number is close to 4 percent, then we are already close to the 5 percent number we are looking for. We'll talk more about income investing in Chapter 8.

2. **5 percent rate with zero interest.** Assume you have your retirement reservoir sitting in cash and yielding almost nothing (let's assume 0 percent per year). Just taking 5 percent at a 0 percent interest rate, the funds will still last you *20 years*. A level 5 percent withdrawal per year × 20 years = 100 percent of your funds withdrawn, and then the money is gone. This gives you two decades of using 5 percent of your overall portfolio as an income source—not bad.

    But certainly not good enough. What if you have 30 or 40 years in retirement? And what if you want to leave something to your children? (Stow that inheritance question back in the overhead bin for now. We'll pull it out later in this chapter).

Factor #1 (using income investing to generate some return each year on your portfolio reservoir) is crucial to the 1,000-Bucks-a-Month Rule, because it allows your money a good chance of lasting a retirement lifetime rather than running out in 20 years.

If you have a portfolio yield of 4 percent (dividends and interest only) and the portfolio experiences even a little bit of growth/appreciation, then **a 4 percent yield plus 1, 2, or 3 percent in growth over time suggests that you can take out 5 percent almost indefinitely.**

This is stretching William Bengen's famous "4 Percent Rule," which we'll discuss later in this chapter, but it needs to be mentioned now because I'm a big believer that this is the way people should plan. It hinges on the income part of income investing.

Quite frankly, the 1,000-Bucks-a-Month Rule is one of the great highlights of this book. In fact, as complicated as financial planning can be—with so many variables, so many moving parts, and all the time involved—this easy-to-follow bit of wisdom can help you remember why you need to save money in the first place. You're saving money so that it can one day replace the income stream you'll be losing when you stop working.

Wall Street's Soufflé Model Has Deflated

If you were paying attention during the 1980s and 1990s, you're familiar with the once "in vogue" Wall Street retirement model, otherwise known as the "soufflé model."

- When the money swells, take out a chunk and wait for it to swell again.
- Your growth averages 8 to 10 percent.
- You live off of 5 to 6 percent of your money, and 20 to 30 years later, you still have more than when you started.

During the bull market of the 1980s and 1990s, the common Wall Street strategy was to think of your retirement money as a soufflé that would swell over time. It was based on the notion that the market would grow at an average of 8 to 10 percent per year.

Wall Street advised you to live off of 5 to 6 percent per year and promised your money would continue to grow and grow. The market had been so good for so long, it was as if there were some super force that protected the soufflé from deflating.

Unfortunately, with two recessions and one major financial crisis over the past 14 years, it's safe to say the soufflé model has deflated—in a big way.

The soufflé model really only worked when you had growth in a relatively steady way. Where this philosophy falls short is when you have a market that goes sideways for extended periods of time, or one that craters and then recovers repeatedly. The only thing steady about a market like this is that you steadily want to pull money out!

For example, what if you were invested in the S&P 500 during one of the two instances (2000 and 2007–2008) when we had corrections of close to 50 percent? This meant your money got cut in half, then recovered roughly 100 percent, then got cut in half again, and then again recovered 100 percent (as of 2013).

These wild, volatile swings create a few soufflé imperfections.

- **The arithmetic of loss:** When you lose 10 percent, you have to make over 11 percent if you want to get back to even. When you lose 25 percent, you have to make over 33 percent to get back to even. When you lose 50 percent, you have to make 100 percent before your portfolio value is fully recovered. See Illustration 5.1.

- If you are pulling chunks of money out from the soufflé corpus to live on, what will you do when your portfolio takes a huge dip during retirement? You end up stuck in a hole, digging another hole, which just compounds the problem.

Since it's no secret a bull market can always lose its horns, I want you to forget about the big swell and sweet smell of soufflés

illustration 5.1   The Arithmetic of Loss

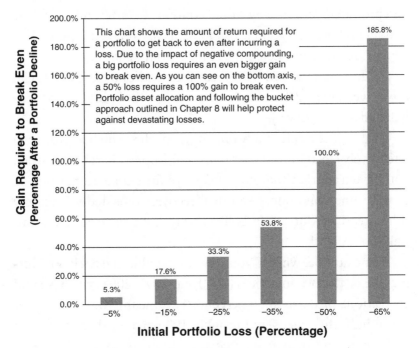

This chart shows the amount of return required for a portfolio to get back to even after incurring a loss. Due to the impact of negative compounding, a big portfolio loss requires an even bigger gain to break even. As you can see on the bottom axis, a 50% loss requires a 100% gain to break even. Portfolio asset allocation and following the bucket approach outlined in Chapter 8 will help protect against devastating losses.

Every time your portfolio suffers a hit, your loss is compounded, making it increasingly difficult to recoup the money you've lost.

and start thinking about your retirement as an income-producing engine.

Going back to the 1,000-Bucks-a-Month Rule: remember that for every $240,000 you save you can expect to have about $1,000 a month at your disposal during retirement (this assumes you wait until age 60 to review). But you want to retire early, right? That's the whole reason you bought this book.

I have good news for you: even if you retire before your sixties, this wonderful rule of thumb will help you target how much you really need to save by giving you a helpful, reliable benchmark. Think of it as a way to forecast that extra stream of income your savings will provide.

4 Percent Rule

I'm going to give you a bit of history on the 4 Percent Rule. In the early 1990s, financial planner William Bengen declared that retirees could deduct 4 percent from their portfolios every year (in addition to adjusting up for inflation) and not run out of money for *at least* 30 years. Analysts and academics verified Bengen's data and supported his assertion.

All a savvy retiree had to do was have a mix of 60 percent stocks and 40 percent bonds, live on 4 percent or so each year (again, adjusting for inflation), and never have to worry about running out of money. So, a retiree with a $1 million nest egg could live on $40,000 a year for 30 years and never have to consider getting a job as a Walmart greeter.

Recently, the *Wall Street Journal* suggested the 4 Percent Rule may no longer stand—this despite the recent highs achieved by the Dow Jones Industrial Average. Perhaps you heard the collective gasp when that headline dropped.

The *Journal* pointed out that, while the Dow has soaring to record heights, growth has been sluggish over the past decade-plus. The Dow hit 11,405 on December 23, 1999. By February 1, 2013 the Dow was at 14,009, only 22.8 percent higher (not including stock dividends).

I hate to take issue with the venerable *WSJ* and the arguably even-more-venerable William Bengen, but I believe the 4 Percent Rule still holds true—for those using their portfolios as income-generating engines. Remember, if you can live on just the income produced by dividends, interest, and distributions produced by your investments—you don't need to worry about how long your principal will last. It will outlive you.

True, we are currently in a period of more muted returns for the major stock averages. Even with the banner year for U.S. stocks in 2013, the Dow was still only 43 percent higher over the preceding 14 years (or about 2.6 percent per year), and 10-year government bonds are paying less than 3 percent per year. But a well-crafted income-focused portfolio consisting of stocks, bonds, real estate investment trusts, and preferred stocks can still generate a yield or "cash flow" of 4 percent.

If we experience even moderate growth in the stock market over the next decade, such portfolios should grow *beyond* that 4 percent cash flow. So, 10 years from now, a larger nest egg should be able to produce a higher level of income while still using 4 percent as a benchmark.

This is how your income should, over time, be able to keep pace with inflation. This is why I still believe the "4 Percent Rule" has legs. Here are some examples, as of April 2014, of diversified investments that are right in the important 4 percent range (just in annual income):

- XLU Utilities Select Sector ETF: 3.55% yield
- AMJ JP Morgan MLP Index Fund: 4.82% yield
- DVY iShares Select Dividend ETF: 3.04% yield
- HYG iShares High Yield Corporate Bond ETF: 5.93% yield

The prices for these exchange-traded funds will go up and down, but the amount of income they produce should stay relatively stable. The income, too, is subject to change, but it should have a bias over time to increase.

So, focus on the cash flow or yield part of the investing equation, and you should find the 4 Percent Rule is still alive and well.

Stretching the 4 Percent into 5 Percent

As I mentioned, the 1,000-Bucks-a-Month Rule stretches the 4 percent into 5. Every step up the incremental ladder—$240,000 to $480,000 to $720,000 and so on—means an additional thousand dollars in your retirement life. I can put any amount of money in a bank account at 0 percent and pull out 5 percent of the original value each year, and that account will last me 20 years (5% per year × 20 years = 100%).

So if:

5% per year × $240,000 = $12,000 per year

Then we can take $480,000—one of our increments of $240,000—and plug it into the same equation:

5% per year × $480,000 = $24,000 per year

That means, if you start with $480,000 saved, you could take out $24,000 every year and not run out for 20 years (not counting for inflation). We can use that context to look at this from a couple of different angles.

- **Example 1.** 5% × $240,000 is $12,000 per year. Assume the $240,000 makes *zero* interest or rate of return. It just sits in a Swiss bank account and the Swiss banker sends you a check for $1,000 a month. Well, mathematically that can continue for 240 months (20 years × 12 months) until you have your entire $240,000 back (not accounting for the impact of inflation).
- **Example 2.** 5% × $1.2 million is $60,000 per year or $5,000 per month; $5,000 per month for 240 months = $1.2 million. This would mean you have 240 months (or 20 years) to live off of 5% before you run out. And that's at a *zero* rate of return.

So, if you have a portfolio that's generating a full 4 percent in income, this is where the rubber meets the road. If you're generating 4 percent per year but taking out 5 percent per year, you are technically dipping into your original principal by 1 percent a year.

How long will your money last now that it's being depleted by 1 percent per year? It would take 100 years. If your retirement lasts that long, I need to start asking *you* for advice.

We can do it another way. If, every single year, you generate 4 percent in income and take out 5 percent each year while simultaneously increasing the amount you need by the amount of inflation—how long does your money last?

The answer is 42 years. It's not quite 100, but I think any of us would be more than happy with that number.

The 1,000-Bucks-a-Month Rule is an indispensable planning tool. If you think you're going to need $3,000 beyond social security, pension, rental income, etc., then at the end of the day you're going to have to save $720,000. It's that simple.

I'm not saying that's a small number. I'm not saying it's easy to do. I'm just telling you that, financially, that's how it breaks down.

What If I Get an Inheritance?

Now let's talk about inheritance. At first glance, it's terrible news because someone had to die for you to get it. But from a financial standpoint, it is typically good news. Who wouldn't want a windfall of cash? But listen closely: **an inheritance is not an excuse for you to spend recklessly or change your lifestyle.** It's merely one more stream you can add to the savings pile.

Baby boomers, aka the Luckiest Generation, will inherit some $8.4 trillion in the coming years. Nearly one in five boomers—those born from 1946 to 1965—will share in that pot. Furthermore, 30 percent of "preboomers" (birth dates from 1930 to 1945) expect to receive an inheritance. Fifteen percent of those folks predict they'll be collecting more than $100,000 after the funeral. That's a chunk of change!

If you find yourself the recipient of an inheritance, keep the following things in mind:

- **Patience.** Don't feel like you need to do something right away. Wait six months to clear your head, and don't make any rash financial decisions. Even if this means leaving the money in an ultra-low yielding but relatively safe place like a money market account for 3, 6, or even 12 months while you develop an overall game plan, that's okay.
- **Don't let it change your life.** Whether you've inherited one dollar or $1 million, it's important to live your daily life as if you didn't receive a dime. It shouldn't impact or alter your lifestyle, but rather be an accelerator to retiring sooner than you think. Think of it as a nice way to pad your savings, eliminate debt, or add to a retirement or college fund.

    If you've been paying attention, you know increasing your savings doesn't give you carte blanche to splurge and spend recklessly—it means more income in the future. Don't think of that inheritance as a windfall of cash. Think of it in terms of the 1,000-Bucks-a-Month Rule. If you inherited $240,000, you'll have an extra 1,000 bucks a month once you retire. Did your parents bequeath you $480,000? Great—make that $2,000 a month in retirement. What it *doesn't* mean is that you can go out and buy a Lexus. Save that Lexus for when you're about to retire.
- **Protect the kids.** Got kids? Want to share the wealth? Slow down, partner. I strongly advise you to make your children wait for their portion of the inheritance. Many adults can't be trusted to do the smart thing with a pot of money, so just imagine how a teenager would behave with a wallet full of cash.

Make a note: When you write or update your will, specify that any money left to minors be used only for education expenses until the recipients reach a certain age. It's for their own good (whether they believe it or not).

Making the Right Choice: Pension Versus Lump Sum

The current temperature of the economy is causing many companies to offer their employees the option of a lump-sum payout, rather than collecting the pension payments they were originally promised. It's a hard decision for people to make, especially with that big pile of money staring them in the face. Here's an easy checklist to help you navigate the decision:

- Take your monthly amount and multiply it by 12.

    Example: $2,000 × 12 = $24,000 a year

- Divide that number into the total amount of the lump sum being offered.
- If the number you come up with equals 6 or 7 percent of the lump sum being offered, consider keeping the pension.
- If the number you come up with is below 6 or 7 percent of the lump sum being offered, consider taking the lump sum and creating income by investing it.

My Data Comes Straight from You!

Hank and Gabrielle are a retired couple living in Elmont on Long Island, New York. When asked if they considered themselves the happiest retirees on the block, they mulled the idea

over. "Everyone else on our block is miserable," they replied
with that quintessentially feisty New York accent. "So we probably are."

As Elmont is a working-class community, the cost of living is
lower than, say, downtown Atlanta. Therefore, the 1,000-Bucks-
a-Month Rule would go a long way for Gabrielle and Hank.
"Someone in Elmont could live quite well," Gabrielle said with
a twinkle in her eye. "Quite well."

This brings up a point I think is important. Despite my
profession, I am not just a financial being. I have a heart, and
I care about the happiness of others. There is the skepticism
that financial advisors, those being paid to manage money, are
constantly focused on telling you to save more. Fair enough. I
get that.

But remember that the information I'm giving you in this
book is based on the answers of real people in 46 states across
the United States. My data comes straight from them. They're
telling me that a liquid net worth of $500,000 (as a minimum) is
the level that needs to be reached to be happy retirees.

You might find yourself thinking, "Doesn't that seem like a
lot of money?" Sure it does—if you think of it as one lump sum.
Instead, think of it as the result of saving $20,000 to $30,000
every year for 40 years. To know how much you should be spending, saving, and earmarking for taxes, simply adopt my TSL
approach.

Divide Your Money into TSL:
Taxes, Savings, Life

The TSL approach is an easy way to split your money into three
separate categories. I want to encourage my readers—especially
those in their twenties and thirties—to strive for the following
percentage breakdown of every dollar they earn:

- Taxes = 30% to the fed and state
- Savings = 20% to a 401(k) plan or to pay down debt
- Life = 50% for food, housing, fun, and everything else

The trick is essentially for people to learn to live on *half* of their gross salary from the very first day of their very first job—and they'll be thankful they started early in life. How can you achieve this? By following my TSL guidelines.

Taxes: 30 Percent

Pro golfer Phil Mickelson found himself in hot water when he complained about 62 percent of his earnings going toward taxes. Few of us feel sorry for a guy who makes close to $50 million a year. But his complaints weren't far off the mark, even though CNBC reported his estimate was a little high.

Consider the new federal tax bracket: nearly 40 percent on families with annual incomes north of $450,000. Add California's 13 percent income tax, and you almost start to feel sorry for Lefty. *Almost.*

Taxes take a huge bite out of all our paychecks. So budget 30 percent of your income for taxes. However, if you are a prodigious earner—$250,000 or more a year, you should budget somewhere between 30 and 40 percent. Furthermore, the really high-earning households, like Phil Mickelson's, should budget closer to 50 percent. That extra 5 to 20 percentage tax bite will just have to come from a reduction of spending.

Remember that I'm talking about an overall "effective" tax rate, so if you're in the 25 percent bracket, it doesn't mean you pay a full 25 percent in federal taxes. The 25 percent comes from adding taxes for social security, Medicare, state income taxes, etc. Follow this and you'll have a good sense of what's left for your savings and life buckets.

Think You Know Your Tax Rate? Think Again

Do you know how much you really pay in taxes? I'm talking about all your taxes: income, capital gains, property, and sales taxes. Most people I ask tell me they pay about 30 percent.

That may sound high, but it turns out to be right. And part of it has to do with your state of residence.

When I gauge a client's approximate overall effective tax rate, I often go to the bankrate.com tax calculator (google Bankrate 1040 tax calculator). You may be surprised to see how low your "effective" federal tax rate is.

But it's probably not your actual tax rate. Most tax calculators don't show all the areas that take a hefty chunk out of your paycheck. FICA and state income taxes are two of the big eaters at the paycheck buffet.

Here's what I mean:

Let's say the Joneses earn $110,000 a year and live in Georgia. Although their overall effective rate is only about 15 percent, the bankrate.com tax calculator more accurately indicates their tax bracket is 25 percent. That's because our tax system is progressive; you pay a higher percentage on your earnings as they go up and pass certain thresholds.

So 15 percent now seems like a pretty good deal. And, for most of you lucky retirees, 15 percent is actually representative of what you pay overall. As you will see in a minute, retirees typically get to stop paying social security taxes, Medicare taxes, and in many places around the country, they get a break on state and local taxes, too.

But let's say the Joneses are still working. Now, for the Joneses and for those of you who are still working and earning a wage, 15 percent is just the tip of the iceberg.

Enter FICA, the 1935 Federal Insurance Contributions Act that established the tax-funded Social Security program. For 2014, the FICA tax is 6.2 percent on the first $117,000 you earn as an individual. So for the Joneses, making $110,000 and in the 25 percent bracket, we have to factor in an additional 6.2 percent tax burden. And, we pay another 1.45 percent tax on everything we earn for Medicare.

Let's Do the Math

We started at 15 percent, then added 6.2 percent for FICA, and then added another 1.45 percent to reach a grand total of 22.65 percent. That means 22.65 cents of every dollar the Joneses earn go toward taxes.

I love living in Georgia—as I'm sure the Joneses do, too—but it's not a cheap state.

Georgians pay 6 percent income tax. (Georgians older than 62 likely pay less, as some state income tax exemptions begin to phase in).

Okay, back to our calculators. Let's add that 6 percent to the 22.65 percent we came up with earlier. We're now at almost 29 percent. That means nearly one-third of every dollar you earn goes toward taxes!

Use the TSL (Taxes, Savings, Life) approach in this chapter for an easy way to budget, live, and stay clean with the IRS.

Savings: 20 Percent

For many years, Vanguard recommended saving between 8 and 12 percent of your gross income to have enough for retirement. Recently, it upped that guideline to 12 to 15 percent, thanks to lower return expectations in the future. I advise clients to try to save 20 percent of their gross income.

Twenty percent is a significant number, but take into consideration the many tax-advantaged ways to save—such as a 401(k),

403(b), 457, or a SEP IRA—and you can get there a lot faster than you might think. Which means, of course, you might be able to *retire* a lot faster.

If 20 percent seems unrealistic right now, just start somewhere and work up to it. Time takes time—and so does saving money.

Life: 50 Percent

Now we're at the truly discretionary spending. The remaining 50 percent (adjust according to my tax advice above) of your income goes here. Spending just 50 percent of your income during your working years on living (food, shelter, transportation, insurance, kid-related costs, entertainment, and the like) will allow you to maintain your lifestyle once you retire.

For Mickelson, who would need to budget about 30 percent for spending, that means limiting his "life" spending to about $15 million a year. Is a single tear streaming down your cheek? I didn't think so.

My TSL formula may seem harsh at first, but you'll get the hang of it. I never said retiring early wouldn't require a little hard work and sacrifice. Just remember to take it one step at a time.

The Power of Saving Early

It was Benjamin Franklin who said, "A penny saved is a penny earned." As important and accurate as he is, I think I can improve on that bit of Founding Father wisdom by adding, "And a penny saved today is worth a lot more pennies than a penny saved tomorrow."

You know you should be saving for retirement right now, but here is yet another reminder of the importance of getting time on your side: If you put $1 away at age twenty, that dollar would be worth $21 by age 65, assuming an average 7 percent return over the years. If you wait until 30 to invest that same $1, it will be worth $10.68. Start at 40 and you will have $5.43. Wait until you turn 50 to invest that same $1 and you'll get a measly $2.76.

So a dollar invested at age 20 is nearly twice as productive as a dollar invested at 30 and *7.5 times* as powerful as a buck that is put to work at age 50!

If you haven't started already, start saving *today*. Every day you wait is costing you serious money. But it's not enough to just save; you need to have a plan to maximize your return. Here's an easy-to-follow five-step plan to get you saving:

1. **Start by creating emergency cash savings.** This should include enough money to pay for anywhere from three to six months of your fixed expenses. Keep these funds in a money market account or other very liquid investments in case you need them immediately. Use this money only for true emergencies, such as job loss or catastrophic medical costs.

2. **If you have a known large expense coming up in the next 12 to 18 months, like a down payment on a house or needing a new roof, set this aside in cash as well.** It doesn't make sense to have your emergency fund wiped out due to a planned financial event, even if it's a year or year and a half away.

3. **Make the maximum contribution to your employer's matching 401(k) program.** While not all companies offer this, a typical matching program is 50 percent of the first 6 percent of your income saved. Find out if your company offers this type of program and what percentage it offers so you can take full advantage of this great benefit.

4. **Next, start funding a Roth IRA.** Contributions are made with after-tax dollars and can be withdrawn

at any time without penalty. Once you reach 59 and a half, all withdrawals are tax-free, and there is no mandatory distribution age.

5. **Once you've funded your Roth IRA, go back and try to max out your 401(k) if possible.** In 2014, the max contribution was set at $17,500 (plus an additional "catch up" amount of $5,500 if you are age 50 or above).

If you've done all of the above and still have money to save, lucky you! Take those funds and put them in a brokerage account pronto.

Romantic Partner Funding: Don't Go It Alone

Getting down on one knee and asking your beautiful lady to help you share in the growth of your nest egg might not sound romantic to her, but as a financial planner, it makes my knees buckle.

There's no way around it: marriage is more economically efficient and cost-effective. Financially, a marriage is about economies of scale. If you have two people adding money to a retirement fund, it grows a lot faster. This is a big reason why so many of the happiest retirees are married.

Whether you have a wife or a domestic partner, you have "someone else" who is chipping in. More hands make lighter work. More jobs mean more income, and that means more savings. It's not easy to get to $500,000. It's not easy to get to $1 million. It takes time. It takes effort. It's an absolute marathon for most people. Why not make it a relay instead?

You might be reading this book and saying to yourself, "This sounds really hard!" You're damn right it's hard. But having a partner in that journey helps a whole heck of a lot. A marriage is about love, romance . . . and two incomes. Why not make the most of it?

If You're Pound-Wise, You Can Afford
to Be Penny-Foolish

One of my biggest pet peeves is the notion that your latte habit is the reason you aren't a millionaire. "For the price of a latte a day, you could save enough money to be a millionaire" is a cliché that's been thrown around willy-nilly in the financial advising world.

I disagree. If you like lattes, buy them! Life is too short to live with a deprivation lifestyle mentality. I am not a fan of one pretentious person telling another person what he or she should spend money on.

The guy who scoffs at the Porsche driver but owns five horses on his organic farm might actually end up spending more money being rustic and humble over the course of those horses' lives than the Porsche driver does on his car. Who is he to judge?

I don't care what you do with your money—as long as you use TSL correctly and the discretionary money is going toward a life that is full of core pursuits. We know that the more hobbies you have, the happier you will be with your life. If being a latte connoisseur is a passion, go for it.

It was George Bernard Shaw who, in *Pygmalion*, wrote, "Happy is the man who can make a living by his hobby."[2] I believe that, except I recast "hobbies" as "core pursuits." I also believe it is the core pursuit itself that gives you life. Getting more pursuits—cultivating and expanding the many enrichments in your life—now *that's* what I want you to spend your money on.

I don't care about what you put in your Starbucks cup—and no one else should, either. In recent years, Americans have become more and more self-righteous about where they spend their money. One person feels his hobby is okay to spend money on, but the hobby his neighbor, cousin, or Uncle Jack engages in is "a waste." I do not like this trend. Uncle Jack is doing what he needs to do fundamentally—it's for him to decide.

Here's what I say: If you are pound-wise, you can afford to be penny-foolish. You can spend your pennies on whatever you want, as long as you get the big things right. What are the big things? Getting to that $500,000-to-million-dollar range, paying yourself first in your retirement plan, saving 20 percent per year. If you can do that, then you can fiddle away your pennies in any way you want and feel good about it.

The happy retiree feels good and proud about what she is spending her money on, and she's not going to judge you for what you're spending your money on.

One of the reasons I love my TSL guidelines is because they take away the guilt factor. As long as you are hitting your numbers, you no longer have to worry about what society deems wasteful. If you are within your budget, and an Iced Vanilla Buttercup Triple Diple Mocha Latte makes you happy—you have a green light to buy it and *enjoy* it!

Fundamentally sound spending and savings habits—TSL—can make you the master of your own choices. Start following this advice today so you no longer have to drink that latte in a dark alley away from society's judgmental gaze.

I want you to think of your money as a living, breathing thing. Remember the tree in the Shel Silverstein story, and don't be that boy. Make the right choices. Use my TSL guidelines and don't get greedy. Trust that, if you plan well and save judiciously, your tree will produce enough fruit to provide for an early retirement—and bless you with an abundance of happy.

Careers That Can Maximize Your Income

My wife was a nurse for years, and nurses are a wonderful part of our economy. However, jobs like nursing, teaching, or government work—where you literally punch a clock and hope for a small raise of 1.5 to 2 percent—make it very difficult to ever accelerate your savings plan in the hopes of retiring early. You're at the mercy of the system. You have no control of the upside of your income.

If you are looking to ensure there is a high ceiling to what you can earn, consider the following careers:

- **Engineers.** Nearly all kinds, from aeronautics, to mechanical, to petroleum, etc.
- **Technology.** Tech startups can have great upside, from software developers, network engineers, user interface designers, etc.
- **Professional services.** Accountants, attorneys, doctors, dentists.
- **Business owner.** In nearly every field (insurance firms, investment firms, even a photography business can be lucrative if you own it).
- **Commercial real estate.** Tenant rep, property development, property management.
- **Pilots and airline mechanics**
- **Consultants.** From technology, to management, to strategy, to tax, etc.

Many of these careers offer significant earnings upside and can range from $100,000 a year to well over $1,000,000.

Making TSL Work for You

Below I've included a simple worksheet to help you apply the TSL formula to your life and savings. First, tabulate your monthly income below, including every single dollar you earn.

Salary   _____
Wages   _____
Tips   _____

Rental income   _____
Trust Fund Income   _____
Under-the-table income   _____
Miscellaneous   _____
Total Income =   _____

Now, apply the following formula:

Total Income × 30% =   _____ **in Taxes**
Total Income × 20% =   _____ **in Savings**
Total Income × 50% =   _____ **for Life**

And there you have it. It's that easy: earmark the top line for taxes, keep the second line in savings, and spend the last line on anything you want.

CHAPTER 6

Secret #3

Pay Off Your Mortgage in as Little as Five Years

Henry Grand paid off his mortgage on a Monday and retired that Tuesday. True story—I'm not making this up. If you want tips on how to be happy in retirement, Henry's your man.

I've worked with Henry for a long time now, so we know each other pretty well. He worked for 40 years, and his wife, the lovely Ava Grand, worked for 25, starting as soon as the last of the kids got off the parent dole. Henry made between $80,000 and $120,000 per year—not a "1 percenter," but he did fine.

He had the opportunity to take a retirement package when he was 64, but it required making five extra installments in order to pay off his mortgage concurrently. What was our advice?

Do it, Henry! Do it!

Why do I feel it's so important to turn your mortgage into ancient history? Sooner or later, every homeowner asks if he

should or shouldn't and is bombarded with a variety of complicated, hedged responses.

Let me offer the simplest possible answer: Yes. **If you are
anywhere near retirement and can afford to pay off your mortgage,
do it.**

All the successful retirees I've known—the folks who are living their dreams—have eliminated or dramatically reduced their
mortgage payment before pressing the retirement button. Paying
off a mortgage by the time you retire will bring you enormous
peace of mind by dramatically reducing the amount of income
your nest egg must produce to create a sunny-side-up retirement.

The data from my survey brooks no objections: happiness
levels rise undeniably as mortgages vanish. And why not? A mortgage, at its simplest, is a large amount of debt. Who *wouldn't* be
happier without that hanging over their heads?

It can be hard for unhappy retirees to see the light at the end
of the tunnel when it comes to paying off their homes. Here they
are getting close to, or in the middle of, retirement, yet they are
still trying to find new ways to pay for the mortgage. This means
they aren't spending money on the things they really want to be
buying. It's all going toward nondiscretionary items and items
you have no choice in paying, the mortgage being the largest. It's
easy to see why this would make someone unhappy.

Flying in the Face of Conventional Mortgage Wisdom

While I have a very strong conviction that paying off the mortgage
leads to happiness in retirement, not everyone shares my opinion.

Conventional wisdom says that if you can earn a higher rate
of return on your investments in the stock market than you are
paying in interest cost on your mortgage, then you should keep
the mortgage—and not pay it off early. Say you are paying 5

percent on a mortgage and you're in the 25 percent tax bracket. The net interest cost of your mortgage is about 4 percent. If you can earn 5 or 6 percent or higher through your investments, why pay off the mortgage with funds that could be earning a higher rate of return than you are paying in interest, right?

Ric Edelman is a big proponent of this line of thinking. A *New York Times* best-selling author, he has written extensively about the financial benefits of keeping a mortgage, and his argument is very compelling. He scrutinizes paying off the mortgage and implores you to invest that money, in order to earn a higher rate of return.

Let's say you owe $100,000 on your house, and you have that money available in after-tax savings. The bank is charging you 4 percent on your mortgage. Rather than pay it off to avoid the 4 percent, Edelman wants you to put that $100,000 in the stock market and make 8 percent on it. Logical argument.

Simple analogy. Simple terms. If I pay off the $100,000, I make $4,000 by not paying that interest on my mortgage. But if I put it in the market instead, I can make $8,000. Subtract $4,000 from the $8,000 and I'm still up $4,000. Good times, right?

Not so fast, Mr. Edelman.

What if the stock market doesn't go up for a year or two . . . or three or four or five? What if it ends up being relatively flat for a decade, like it was in the 2000s? You wake up one day and realize you've been paying interest on your mortgage but your stock market investments haven't been holding up their end of the bargain. Where do you come out then? Not $4,000 ahead as the theory would have you believe. The stock market doesn't kowtow to theory. If it did, a lot more people would be driving Bentleys, believe you me.

The average investor is not making a steady 8 percent per year, so why would we advise people to trust the market rather than paying off their mortgages? Furthermore, in "real life," most people don't have 100 percent of their money in stocks, and those who do probably end up timing the stock market poorly. It is widely understood in field of behavioral finance, that over time most individual investors typically end up with returns far less than what a particular average does (i.e., REITs, U.S. stocks, international stocks).

With that in mind, advising people to not pay off something that is costing them a known 4 or 5 percent (and in many times over history, higher than that) and betting on the unknown possibility of 8 percent is an argument that falls on deaf ears for me. I just don't buy it.

Benefits of Paying Off the Mortgage

Now, here's what I *do* buy: that paying off your mortgage will make you a whole lot happier in retirement. Consider the following two benefits, for starters:

- **It's obvious—you are no longer paying interest to the bank.** Didn't the Aflac duck tell us that saving is the same as earning? Or was it Howard the Duck? I'm mixing up my mallards, but that won't stop me from keeping your mortgage ducks in a row. In fact, in this case saving is even better than earning because at some point you will be making interest on the money you save. Now that's what I call a golden goose!
- **Paying off your mortgage gives you the budgetary freedom to spend more money on finding purpose and happiness in life.** I don't know about you, but I don't find much purpose in cutting a check to Wells Fargo. Whether it's travel or volunteering, mountain cycling or Scottish games, you should be spending your money on the things that give you purpose and happiness.

No matter how much you love your home, remember that the mortgage payment is still just *money for shelter*. And while that turn of phrase sounds like it would be the title of a cool Rolling Stones song, it isn't.

The One-Third Rule: If It Applies to You, Write a Check Today

If I'm not paying that mortgage note anymore, it lowers my spending tremendously and puts less pressure on my overall financial plan. Think of your retirement assets as an engine. You're no longer working, so that engine has to function with the finite amount of oil already in it. No more oil changes at the Jiffy Lube. Every thousand dollars you spend revs your retirement engine another thousand RPM. With the mortgage payment being the biggest expense, you're spending thousands of dollars more a month—and are in danger of redlining the engine.

The more RPM, the more things have to go right in order for your engine not to crack. Yet here you are spending possibly up to nine grand a month. Not even Mr. Goodwrench could keep that engine from cracking. Get rid of that mortgage before it's too late!

What no one else talks about when giving mortgage advice is the psychological burden that comes along with having a mortgage, and the subsequent release people feel when they've paid it off. I can crunch the numbers as well as the next guy, but if you walk into my office or call into my radio show and ask why you should pay off a mortgage with funds that could be earning a higher rate of return than the outflow of interest payments, I look you square in the eye—even if it's via radio waves—and tell you straight: the happiest retirees care more about happiness than risking engine failure for just a few more shekels.

Of course, the answer to the mortgage question will be different for people in different stages of life and people who have different tolerances to investment risk. But as you think about your mortgage, consider the following rule:

The One-Third Rule: If you can pay off your mortgage using no more than one-third of your nonretirement savings, consider writing that check today. If, for example, you owe $40,000 on your home and have $150,000 in savings, *not* including your 401(k) and/or IRA funds, eliminating the mortgage lifts a burden and leaves you plenty of cushion for unexpected expenses. Let's say your mortgage balance is $150,000 and you have $300,000 in nonretirement investments. Now, you could pay off the mortgage in a lump sum. But it would deplete your nonretirement assets by a full 50 percent. And subsequently wipe out a huge portion of your "liquid assets" that can also serve as a cash cushion. That's too much of a hit, and in this case I would advise against it.

Your mortgage interest rate is inevitably higher than the interest CDs or short-term bonds will give you. This may give comfort to some conservative investors: If you are a very conservative investor who prefers the stability and reliability of CDs and short-term government bonds to the volatile S&P 500 stock index, you may want to drastically accelerate your mortgage payoff. CDs and bonds will almost certainly earn *less* than the rate you are actually paying on your mortgage. So there is little to no advantage to keeping money in an account earning less than 1 percent when you are paying 5 percent on your mortgage balance.

Disciplined investors can wait. For those who would still prefer putting $200 into a mutual fund each month, rather than paying an extra $200 on the mortgage, that's okay—as long as you are disciplined about it.

Oftentimes investors who choose not to accelerate their mortgage payments in lieu of investing elsewhere end up failing to invest it elsewhere, putting them right back on track to Unhappy City. I'm all for putting an extra $200 toward your favorite Vanguard dividend-paying stock ETF, but just don't let it fall through the cracks. As much as I want that mortgage paid off, it's not a good idea to head into retirement with a house fully paid for at the expense, no pun intended, of having no money in the bank. Last time I checked, you can't pay for groceries with shingles from the roof.

Paying Off the Mortgage Gives You a Break

For those nearing retirement, paying off the mortgage creates what I call a *deflationary moment* in their financial planning. Think about all the financial outflow in your life. Are any of those prices going down? Colleges are getting more expensive; healthcare is getting more expensive. Gas, cars, land, daycare, food, milk, eggs, coffee beans are all getting more expensive by the day.

With all this inflation in our lives, when do you get a chance to see any deflation? Give a guy a break, right?

Paying off your mortgage *is* that break. You're deflating the amount of money that has to go out the window, and it's something that lasts forever, which is a very powerful and positive psychological force. Knowing that the bank can't touch the dwelling in which you hang your hat feels damn good.

I've learned from the happiest retirees that there is a certain amount of calm and security in the cushion of knowing your house is your house, free and clear. If you want to join the ranks of the happy retirees, you've got to pay off the mortgage. Look at Illustration 6.1.

I want to reiterate: the number of years to pay off the house goes down as the amount of happiness goes up. On average, happy retirees have their mortgage payoff date within sight— roughly 10 years, and often closer to 5.

In contrast, the unhappiest retirees have somewhere between 11.5 and 12 years left on their mortgage. So, the closer you are

Illustration 6.1   Years Until Mortgage Is Paid Off (Mean)

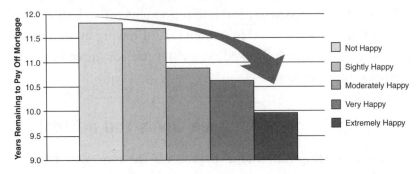

As you can see, the fewer years retirees have left on their mortgage, the happier they tend to be.

to having it paid off, the more likely you are to be happy. Some of the factors are tangible, some aren't, but from all my years of experience in this field I can tell you that the best move overall is to pay off that mortgage by the time you retire (if you can). The financial and psychological factors both play huge parts.

Morty Shortened His Mortgage Repayment—and So Can You

Let's take a run at this topic from a slightly different angle. If you can't afford to pay off your entire mortgage with one (or a few) large payments, then the best way to approach it is to accelerate your payments each month.

This might be the biggest eye-opener and most realistic way to get rid of your mortgage in practice. Many of the families I work with do it this way and they seem to have good results.

A great way to do this is to go to bankrate.com and use its mortgage payoff calculator.[3] An example is provided for you in Illustration 6.2. This is a man who decided to accelerate his payments and get rid of his mortgage sooner than he thought he could. Let's call him "Morty."

Illustration 6.2   Bankrate Early Mortgage Payoff Calculator

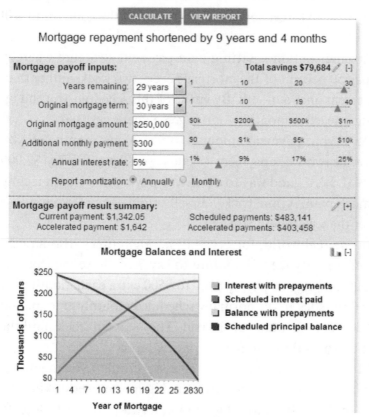

Mortgage payoff calculator

Calculate your payment and more

How much interest can be saved by increasing your mortgage payment? This mortgage payoff calculator helps you find out.

CALCULATE   VIEW REPORT

Mortgage repayment shortened by 9 years and 4 months

Mortgage payoff inputs: Total savings $79,684 ✎ [-]

Years remaining:	29 years ▾
Original mortgage term:	30 years ▾
Original mortgage amount:	$250,000
Additional monthly payment:	$300
Annual interest rate:	5%
Report amortization:	● Annually ○ Monthly

Mortgage payoff result summary: ✎ [+]
Current payment: $1,342.05   Scheduled payments: $483,141
Accelerated payment: $1,642   Accelerated payments: $403,458

Mortgage Balances and Interest   ▮▪ [-]

☐ Interest with prepayments
▨ Scheduled interest paid
☐ Balance with prepayments
■ Scheduled principal balance

Year of Mortgage

By adding $300 to his monthly payment, Morty shortened his repayment by nine years and four months. He got a whole decade of his life back!

In this example, Morty has just started his 30-year mortgage in the amount of $250,000. His **APR**, or annual interest rate, is 5.0 percent. His regular monthly scheduled payment is $1,342. If he adds $300 to that payment each month, he will shave 9 years and 4 months off the life of the loan. That will save Morty a grand total of $79,684—not too shabby.

You know when you're working out and you don't look at the clock, and so you "accidentally" run five extra minutes on the treadmill? You just burned a bunch of calories without even knowing it. That's how it is with paying your mortgage. You simply have to forget about the sacrifice, and the good result will be headed your way.

Another option is setting up a payment structure whereby you pay 50 percent of the mortgage every two weeks rather than 100 percent once a month. By virtue of this schedule, you end up paying one extra monthly mortgage payment per year.

So, if your payment amounts to $2,000 per month and you opt for the two-week payment schedule, you'll pay an extra $2,000 that year. It's a good way to accelerate payments without feeling too much pain. Again, trick yourself into paying off your house sooner than you think you can.

In the real world, for every 10 happy retirees who have to pay off a mortgage, I'd venture to say 7 of those incorporate the methodology of paying $200 to $500 extra each month. The other three stick to the normally scheduled monthly amount and then do the final chunk at the end. They stay on track until the point at which they can handle paying more.

Money is relative to us all. What is painful to you might not be painful to the rich guy with the big house overlooking the ocean in Santa Barbara. (Or to Oprah, who lives next door to him.) Find what works for you.

Do What the Happy People Do

What I'm trying to do is pass on the secrets of very happy and successful retirees. Let me emphasize that not all are wealthy in the traditional sense. We're not talking about multi-multimillion-aires and billionaires—we're talking about the happiest retirees.

You might like what I'm saying and you might not, but you can't argue with the fact that these are behaviors and habits happy retirees have in common. I get my info from my clients, from people who call in to the radio show, and from the answers people gave me in the comprehensive survey I conducted. From all this, it's clear a majority of these happy people no longer have mortgage payments.

Of course, it's possible to be happy with a mortgage. But the percentage of possibility is lower, so why take the risk?

Back in 2009, the happiest retirees weren't as affected by the financial crisis as the unhappy group—and their lack of a mortgage played a big part. In the midst of the financial crisis, with the economy in recession, there was a big fear about real estate, and a tremendous amount of underwater property. Too many people owned "too much house" and had too little equity. Debt was in abundance.

However, retirees in the happy group had a different financial forecast. They would come into my office and say "Oh, we just have one house, and it's paid off." Or, "We've got $30,000 to $50,000 left and then we're done. We're 55 years old and hoping to get this paid off in the next three or four years."

I heard this over and over again. I thought I just had a funny coincidence on my hands, but it happened so many times that finally I couldn't ignore it. I realized there had to be some kind of pattern here because these people were happy and comfortable with where they stood in life, despite the fact that we were right in the middle of the financial crisis—a very dark period in our nation's economic history. The more I researched it, the more I couldn't deny that paying off the mortgage really did give these people a cushion, offering them greater happiness and overall peace of mind.

Balancing IRA Money and Non-IRA Money in the Mortgage Payoff Game

Let's say I owe $100,000 on my house. I have $500,000 in my IRA and $200,000 in my after-tax account. I can't touch my IRA without getting punched in the face by taxes, so I'd be paying my mortgage out of the bucket with $200,000. Should I pay my mortgage or not?

The answer in this case is no. After I pay off the house, I'd only be left with $100,000 in my after-tax account. This means my liquidity is 50 percent less than it was. I don't want to go into retirement with such a low amount of nonretirement money available to me. Yes, I have $500,000 in my IRA, but to access that money I have to pay taxes. Not fun, right? It gets worse.

You almost never want to take money out of a regular/traditional IRA to pay off a mortgage because every nickel you pull out of that IRA is considered taxable income. It might as well be income from a paycheck because it counts toward your adjustable gross income in the same way.

If I have to pull money out of the IRA to pay off a $100,000 mortgage and I'm in a 20 percent tax bracket, I'm going to end up having to pull $125,000 out to account for the taxes owed ($125,000 − 20% in taxes = $100,000). This is called *an income and tax escalation phenomenon.*

To net the $100,000 I needed, I had to pull out $125,000 to pay the mortgage, and the oh-so-friendly IRS is happy I did because not only is it taxable; it looks like more income and pushes me into an even higher tax bracket. Now I'm paying taxes on the money *and* paying a higher tax percentage overall. I got chewed up and spit back out. You can see why it's so important not to take money out of the retirement fund to pay off the mortgage!

In order to avoid the real-life version of the hypothetical financial black eye I just gave myself, you have to remember to ask yourself this simple question:

Can I take one-third or less of my after tax money to pay off my mortgage?

If the answer is *yes*, do it.

If the answer is no, don't. Instead, look at accelerating your monthly payments by a few hundred dollars a month like Morty illustrated in Illustration 6.2.

The Flexibility No Mortgage Affords

There are other important aspects to paying off the mortgage before retirement. First of all, you buy yourself some flexibility. If you need an equity line, you can get it. I'm not recommending a reverse mortgage, but you'd have the opportunity to use it if you had to. You'd also have the flexibility of being able to move somewhere else, rent, or even buy a place and not have to carry two mortgages.

The flexibility in your life skyrockets when you pay off your home. Not being financially beholden or burdened is so important. There's a lot of utility in that.

Remember Marilyn Noble from Chapter 4? She's a great example of someone with maximum flexibility. She was able to sell her house and use the money to buy two smaller houses. It's amazing how much you can afford using the equity from a fully paid off home as you head into retirement. Wouldn't you want that kind of flexibility? Here's just a tiny taste of the things I've seen happy retirees transition into:

- A new, smaller home with less maintenance and lower utility bills
- A cabin in the mountains and a lakeside cottage
- A cabin in the mountains and a condo in town—a popular choice for those who can afford to avoid traffic in my hometown of Atlanta
- A condo on Lake Michigan and another in the steamy gulf of Florida

- A home near your grandchildren—and another one far away from your grandchildren, for when you need some time away
- An RV to travel across North America
- Enjoying vacations using the vacation rental by owner (VRBO system) described in the next section

Vacation Rentals by Owner: Enjoying a Second Home Without Having to Buy One

There are so many options for vacationing these days, and they allow more opportunity to give up that stressful mortgage payment. My favorite of these is VRBO—vacation rentals by owner, which also operates under the name homeaway.com (so both vrbo.com and homeaway.com will work for you). I'm also a fan of using airbnb.com as well, which also has a vast inventory of homes that you can rent in cities all around the world

Technology and efficiency have led to more affordable lodging and housing in highly valued areas. In today's world, I'm not sure it's necessary to have a second home. A lot of the happiest retirees still do, so it's not a make-or-break situation, but if you want to shed the mortgage payment on that beach or mountain home, VRBO allows you to enjoy vacations without being tied to anything.

There are also vacation clubs, such as Inspirato, where joining allows you *access* to wonderful properties around the world. There are many options at varying price levels and with different incentive packages, but it's safe to say that the much maligned and inflexible timeshare model has evolved to give vacationers more desirable options.

Following are five important things to understand when considering higher-end vacation clubs:

- By and large, they are *not* cheap. They typically involve a one-time, up-front cost of several thousand dollars to more than $15,000, and they can also entail annual membership fees. Make sure you have a list of *all* fees before giving over your hard-earned money.

- The properties you have to choose from are jaw dropping. If you're feeling inspired, spend a few minutes on www.inspirato.com. They're gorgeous!
- The daily cost can range from $500 to more than $1,500 per night—so the costs are jaw dropping, as well. Know that going in.
- Locations range from Aspen to St. Barts to Provence to Tuscany to Thailand to the Turks and Caicos Islands.
- These clubs are about *access*—the perfect setup for happy retirees who have a larger-than-normal travel budget and never want to be tied to one particular destination. Remember how I'm always saying retirement is freedom? Well, at these clubs, they'd agree.

Buy the "Big Stuff" Now, *Before* You Retire

Remember the overall concept that your mortgage is most likely your biggest expense—the biggest potential black hole for your finances. And don't forget that in addition to the mortgage, there is a litany of expensive problems that can go wrong with your home, such as:

- A leaky skylight
- Holes in the roof
- Broken plumbing
- Broken heating or AC
- Warped floors
- An outdated kitchen that "just has to be redone"
- Foundation work (your house needs a new foundation)

All of these are big-ticket items. Your wallet cringes just thinking about them. It would take more than a trip to the local Target or Home Depot to take care of these; you'd have to dust off your yellow pages or get a referral from Kudzu.com to find yourself a handyman or carpenter. And if you think they're inexpensive, allow me to burst your bubble—they aren't. They have an amazing ability to turn a two-hour job into a two-day journey.

I recently had a handyman put in new front porch doors. Not only was there a half-inch gap underneath the door so that you could literally see outside, but when the workers painted they opted to sand the actual glass to remove stray paint splatters. Now I have four brand-new French doors with a gap big enough for a groundhog, and brand-new glass where 10 out of the 40 panes have permanent scratches.

So I went out and found a better handyman: Mr. Rex Gillman.

Rex happens to be one of the funniest individuals I've ever met, so in addition to his talent, he keeps me laughing. He is clad in overalls, and the rogue hairs on his half-bald head yearn for the comb-over from days of yore. If the nutty professor were tailgating at an SEC college football game, that would be Rex. He's loaded with every southern proverb in the language. As Rex would put it, he's got "one foot on the banana peel and the other foot in the grave."

He's a great handyman, but at $50 an hour, I think it's me that has one foot on the banana peel and the other one in the grave. Yet, despite the painful bills I receive, I can handle it because I'm not yet retired. That's the key.

I've had more than one retiree from the happy group tell me that their philosophy is to pay for all the "big stuff" before retirement so it doesn't hit them when they retire. If this seems like common sense to you, that's good! Unhappy retirees don't get it. The bottom line is that if you want to enlist in the army of home repair, you might want to work an extra year and then retire once the deployment is over.

That way, you can have the means to pay off your mortgage on Monday and retire on Tuesday, just like good ol' Henry and Ava Grand.

Four Steps to Paying Off Your Mortgage, Starting Today

To recap, I've outlined my four-step "beat your mortgage" process below:

1. **Keep your mortgage payment below 15 percent of your gross monthly income**—and well below the mortgage industry's conventional mark of closer to 30 percent. The last thing you want to do is rob Peter to pay Paul.

2. **Visit the bankrate.com early mortgage payoff calculator.** This can be a really fun tool—give yourself half an hour and plug in a bunch of different numbers. Try increasing your monthly payments by $50, then $100, then $200, then $500 (just for kicks). Experiment with different combinations. Plug in your own numbers and see how many years (and dollars) can be shaved off by paying an extra couple hundred dollars per month. You may be surprised how easily you can move the meter.

3. **Make biweekly mortgage payments (that's 50 percent of the note every two weeks) instead of 100 percent once a month.** This is an easy trick that's surprisingly effective. Making biweekly mortgage payments will force you to make an entire extra monthly payment per year. You just sneak it right in there.

4. **Remember the One-Third Rule.** When you get to the point where you can pay off the mortgage using one-third (or less) of your after-tax savings, it's time to write that check and bid your naughty mortgage adieu.

Whether you're employing one of these early payoff strategies or a combination of them, you will be able to shave years or perhaps decades off the life of your mortgage. If these strategies get you mortgage-free in five years or less, you're well on your way to retiring sooner than you think.

CHAPTER 7

Secret #4

Develop an Income Stream from Three or Four Sources, Not Just One

Steve Burton is a high-powered senior vice president at a big Fortune 100 media company. You know the type—a motivated executive with a large, steady stream of income that continues to help fill his savings reservoir. Steve has worked since he was 16, and he's done well for himself. He'll be able to retire early, not simply because of his high income, but because he's been a prodigious saver and is taking the necessary steps to be a member of the happy group.

For the last three years, Steve has been training to become certified in timepiece creation and repair. From the Rolex to the Bulova to all the other intricately designed time-telling devices, he's on his way toward a three-year watch specialist certification. It's actually called a CMW21 (Certified Master Watchmaker of the 21st Century), a fascinating designation I would have never known about if not for Steve. It's amazing the things I continue to learn and be exposed to thanks to happy retirees.

But back to Steve. This executive loves watches. Picture Warren Buffett hunched over your mom's Timex, an old but proud sign above his desk that reads, "It took a licking, but I'll get it ticking." It doesn't matter that Steve works in a big fancy office and makes a lot of money. He loves the intricacies, the design, and the systematic genius of watches.

It's become a core pursuit for him. And guess what? It's part-time work. Once he retires from the stressful, high-powered job that's allowed him to accumulate 3.5 million Delta SkyMiles, he'll be ready to start cranking on the watches—no pun intended.

Steve will probably retire around 56 or 57 and work on watches three to four days a week—at his own leisure. He'll make a decent living doing it, probably anywhere from $50,000 to $80,000 per year, to supplement the other financial steps he's already taken to plan his retirement. All the more important: he'll have fun doing it. Imagine that!

What Steve knows—and many others don't—is that the more "rivers" or "streams" of income you have, the happier you'll be. You need to start thinking about this now. Make "multiple streams of income" a mantra and repeat it often.

As usual, the proof is in the data:

- Eighty-five percent of happy retirees have more than one source of income.
- Nearly half of happy retirees have three income sources or more.
- Fifty-seven percent of unhappy retirees report only one source of income.
- The average number of income sources for happy retirees is 2.6.

- The average number of income sources for unhappy retirees is 1.85.

More rivers or streams of income equal happier retirees. It's that simple. In this chapter, we'll discuss how to go about making those rivers flow.

The More Rivers of Money, the Greater Your Reservoir

When it comes to generating income, you want to create as many tributaries as possible to come together in one new, predictable larger stream.

For example: A 63-year-old couple may have access to the following:

- Two monthly checks that come from social security (one for $1,750, one for $1,150)
- One small pension from a past employer for $560/ month
- One part-time income from Home Depot for $1,100/ month
- Investment income from a portfolio of $1,600/month

That's a total of five different income sources that, in aggregate, equate $6,160 a month—or approximately $73,920 a year (pretax). None of these tributaries are enormous in their own right, but together they create a powerful cash flow of over $70,000 a year.

If money were water, would you think of it as a river or a lake? More often than not, I find the answer to this question is different for men than it is for women. A higher percentage of women look at money—savings, investments, income—as a lake.

It's a giant mass that has been created through previous actions. Men seem to think of it as a river—a more fluid entity that continues to flow and change.

Which mentality is the right one to have? They both are. Remember the following: Money is a *river* while you're working and a *reservoir* once you retire.

Let me explain. While you're working, you have one or two big paychecks flowing into a reservoir of "savings." Not all of the money from these paychecks makes it into the reservoir because you need some of it to live, but every year you try to let in as much as you can. The hope is that when you're 55, 60, or 65, you'll have filled the reservoir up high enough to provide much of the drinking water you'll need for the rest of your life.

If you retire from your full-time job, "Paycheck Rio Grande" stops flowing. Most likely your reservoir isn't full enough to keep you hydrated by itself, so you have to figure out a way to begin collecting water from other sources. This is a big transition—both in thinking and in practice—and your willingness to make this transition is a key factor in your ability to become a happy retiree.

Moving Out of the Accumulation Phase and Into Distribution

The dynamics of money and income shift dramatically throughout our lifetimes. Most of our working years are part of the accumulation phase. We accumulate and expand our wealth in the attempt to "sock" money away for retirement.

We expect our money to grow, and that growth comes through appreciation and income generation. If we have mutual funds that pay dividends, those dividends (aka "income") are reinvested and continue to grow and accumulate over time (aka "appreciation"). We're in the accumulation phase from the day we start saving to the day we stop working: in other words, the day we stop receiving our paycheck (or "traditional means" of income)—W-2, 1099, ownership distributions, salaries, bonuses, commissions, fees, etc. So, we have this income flowing in while we're 30, 40, and 50, but it's really a source to facilitate our current lifestyle, and a resource to save for our future lifestyle.

But something drastic happens when we hit retirement. That consistent stream of money stops. In some cases it stops abruptly; in cases where one spouse keeps working longer than the other, it slows to a halt. The point is that in a very short period of time, your traditional income stops. The accumulation has been flowing like a giant river, but now the water has dried up.

Don't panic. We're going to stop thinking about a giant river and start focusing on ways to create multiple smaller tributaries.

This transition is dramatic, and there are few things that provoke as much anxiety as moving from one big river into several smaller streams. Many people began working in their teenage years and have lived most of their lives generating a steady paycheck. Whether they worked for a company or for themselves, they've been generating wage income as long as they can remember—and it can be scary to break that habit.

"I work and therefore money comes in" is the mentality. Now, in retirement, the strategy changes. Rather than grinding it out at the office, you're relying on a variety of other factors to work in your favor. **You're moving out of accumulation and into distribution.** You have to relinquish some control, but if you've prepared, that's not going to be a problem.

Assuming your typical W-2 or 1099 paycheck is no longer flowing, here are some potential sources of income.

- Part-time work
- Social security
- Pension income (state, federal, nonprofit, corporate)

- Rental income
- Investment income

Now let's look at each of these in detail.

Part-Time Work

Atlanta is the Home Depot headquarters of the world. I see many people, both men and women, who are ready to retire from their full-time career but decide they'd like to go work at Home Depot two to three days a week. Some of them are good at fixing stuff, and some love the garden section. For both groups, working part-time at Home Depot adds to their quality of life and brings in a relatively modest stream of income.

Home Depot is only one option. If the idea of part-time work appeals to you, consider the following:

- If you like retail, fill out at an application at Nordstrom, Ann Taylor, or another clothing store at a nearby mall.
- If you're into cars, think about applying at Advanced Auto Parts or Pep Boys.
- If sports are your thing, try a sporting goods store like Dick's or Sports Authority.
- If you enjoy books, apply to work at Barnes & Noble or a local bookstore.
- If you want something high-energy, try Starbucks or your favorite coffee shop.
- If you love your church or temple, see if there's a part-time position available at your place of worship.

The options really are endless!

Some people take on part-time consulting gigs. What better way to make money and stay engaged and active then to continue being paid for some of the same things you were so good at before you retired?

Recently I've been working with Elaine Hill, a woman who was "downsized" from IBM and effectively forced to take early retirement at 59. IBM had been paying her a low to mid six-figure salary—in the ballpark of $130,000 per year. It was a good living but certainly "midrange" for IBM standards. Yet, because of all the benefits that went along with the position, Elaine was considered a "high-cost employee."

As we all know, every so often companies go in and clean out the "high-cost" employees when the budget calls for it. Unfortunately for Elaine, she was the collateral damage of IBM's spring-cleaning. On the upside, she barely had time to pour a second glass of chardonnay before IBM asked her to come back as an independent contractor. Essentially, they offered her the old job back, making an income sans benefits.

Elaine's situation isn't an uncommon one. Many retirees have the option to still bring in a supplemental paycheck once their main career comes to an end. It's less tax efficient, less secure, and includes fewer benefits, but that's okay. Remember: think many small streams, not one big river.

Social Security

Nearly all Americans (if you paid in during your working years) will receive social security payments at some point in their lives. According to the official website, 9 out of 10 individuals 65 and older receive social security benefits.[1]

The unfunded liabilities of the program are no secret—more money is promised to go out than the government has saved in the social security trust fund.

However, social security is not to be scoffed at in terms of your retirement planning. Even with potential changes on the horizon, it is one of the streams you want flowing into your reservoir. I have clients who get as little as $800 a month and others who receive more than $3,000 a month.

The great part about social security is that once it begins, you can rely on the numbers to generally stay about the same, with very modest increases tied to inflation. And whatever the amount, it's still another stream. **Remember: every income stream matters, no matter how small.** The key to money secret #4 is adding as many as you possibly can.

A quick note about some of the commonly understood challenges faced by our Social Security System: There is no secret that the Social Security Trust Fund in the United States is projected to run out of money sometime in the mid-2030s. As recently as November 2013, the chief actuary from the Social Security Administration said that the operating surplus (or Trust Fund) that social security payments come from will not run dry until the year 2033, at which time benefits to retirees will have to be reduced by approximately 23 percent on an ongoing basis. Benefits at that point would be made using a pay-as-you-go system. Social security taxes come into the system from those who are working, then go right back out to those who are retired or promised benefits.

If the trust fund runs out as projected, the amount paid into the system is projected to be about 4.7 percent of GDP per year, while the amount to be paid out is approximately 6.1 percent of GDP. The fix? Simply reallocate about 1.5 percent of GDP toward funding the system. Or delay future benefits a year or two, reduce benefit payments, raise the amount we all pay into the system, or some combination of these efforts. Mathematically the answers may be easy, but the political process will have to run its course before we ultimately come to a long-term solution.

In the meantime, we have about two more decades of uninterrupted service from social security, and in a worst-case scenario (beyond 2033), benefits will be reduced by about 25 percent of what is currently being paid out. These facts are less than comforting, but at least you know what lies ahead and we can plan for it. You can visit www.socialsecurity.gov to find out more.

Pension Income

If you have a pension, congratulations! Many of us don't, including me. Pensions have both a wonderful and tragic history in this country. Is it a legal obligation for your company to pay the pension it has promised you? Yes, but what if the company goes out of business?

I agree with Roger Lowenstein, who wrote about this topic in a 2013 *Barron's* article, in which he stated the tendency of companies to neglect the obligation to keep pension funds solvent "is a pity because, when properly run, pensions remain the best form of retirement plan. They do away with many of the risks born by individuals alone, such as outliving one's savings or retiring at the wrong time."[2] Not to mention, he points out, most people don't have enough expertise or time to manage their own portfolios successfully.

Yes, it's unsettling, but luckily we have the Pension Benefit Guarantee Corporation (PBGC), a U.S. government agency that protects the retirement incomes of more than 40 million American workers in more than 26,000 private-sector defined benefit pension plans. The maximum pension benefit guaranteed by the PBGC is set by law and adjusted yearly. For plans that end in 2013, the maximum guarantee for workers who retire at age 65 is $57,477.24.[3]

In addition to that worry is the fact that one of the most well-documented issues in corporate America is the lack of funding of current pension obligations. There are plenty of examples of this. The same *Barron's* article points out instances from Studebaker to General Motors to the State of Illinois to the city of San Bernardino, California. It seems the overpromise and underdelivery of pensions is almost more of an American pastime than the game of baseball.

Not all pension obligations are upside down, but there's clearly a problem in America: we have underestimated how long people live. Pension programs were put in place decades ago when life expectancies were shorter, and it only stands to reason that with longer life expectancies, those old actuary tables aren't going to add up.

Despite all this, the chances that a pension will change or default are actually very low (not to mention a backstop from the PBGC). So if you have a pension, it's wonderfully useful and reliable, and we will gladly let it flow into that reservoir.

Rental Income

There are two approaches you can take with rental income.

1. Wait for retirement and then use a portion of your nest egg to invest in income-oriented properties.
2. Become an accumulator of rental real estate over time.

I saw a lot of individual investors use the first approach successfully in 2009 and 2010, when real estate prices were depressed. Home prices came down close to 30 percent over a three- or four-year period. Rental demand increased as fewer and fewer people were willing to take on mortgages, so it became financially productive and logical to buy a house for $100,000—if you could generate a monthly rent of at least $833 from it, equaling 10 percent per year on your money.

Does this interest you? Great. Below is a quick-and-easy how-to. You can do either of the following:

- Buy a house for $100,000—in cash, so there's no mortgage payment— generating approximately $10,000 a year in gross rental income (a 10 percent gross yield on the cash you've invested).
- Put some money down (say, 20 percent) and borrow the remaining 80 percent from a bank. As long as you have a reasonable interest rate on the loan, you should still have decidedly positive cash flow from the property.

In both instances, you now have an income-producing property that will pay you monthly cash flow for as long as the house is still standing and you have renters. I have seen countless happy retirees use this methodology and turn a portion of their retirement nest egg into income-producing rental property. (Remember Nick and Katie Benjamin?)

This can be a very effective use for a portion of your retirement nest egg. Not only is it very effective at generating cash flow, it can give you a part-time job managing the properties if you have a few of them. Fixing broken toilets, scheduling air conditioner repairs, patching leaky roofs, making sure the lawn is mowed—all joyous work for those who love to be handy!

Some people really enjoy being a landlord. The Benjamins love it. I work with lots of happy retirees (and aspiring happy retirees) who love it as well. It keeps them busy and keeps another stream of income trickling into the reservoir. Furthermore, it helps solve for the strange, listless no-man's-land some retirees experience when they go abruptly from full-time work to having nothing to do and no income to earn.

The second approach to rental income—and the better way to do it in my opinion—is to become an accumulator of rental real estate over time. The sooner in your life you start accumulating property that generates monthly rental income, the more significant it will be by the time you get to that age of financial independence.

Robert Kiyosaki's *New York Times* bestselling book *Rich Dad, Poor Dad* puts a big focus on rental income. It was really popular in the decade of the 2000s because at that time real estate paid a nice income, and nearly all types of property steadily rose year after year in value. A lot of leverage was involved (meaning borrowed money) but it didn't matter at the time because the real estate market was doing so well. If someone wanted to buy a million dollars' worth of property, he could put down $100,000, borrow the other $900,000, and get all his rental property working for him, paying him a nice 5 to 10 percent in income.

Furthermore, all of the asset values were going up because all of the real estate prices were going up and up and up. Everything was great—until the financial crisis of 2007, 2008, and 2009 hit.

This was the first time in our generation that we saw real estate prices go down, and I don't mean by small figures. Prices fell between 25 to 65 percent, depending on where you lived. Condos that were bought on spec in Nevada and Miami were down 50 to 70 percent.

[Note: Now that we've come through, to some extent, and arrived at the other side of the financial crisis, real estate prices have clearly stabilized. In fact, at the time of writing this book, home values across most of America have been on the rise for the better part of two years and are now comparable to home values in 2004. So, home prices have a long way to go to get back to the levels we saw in 2006–2007, but an environment of flat to slightly higher home prices (like we may be in for the next several years) makes favorable conditions for property owners and landlords alike.]

So taking the earlier example: if I buy a house for $100,000 and get a renter to pay $833 per month, that comes out to exactly $10,000 a year. That's a nice 10 percent (gross yield) if I actually paid cash for it. (Yes, the *net* yield will be lower once I pay for maintenance and taxes and upkeep on the house.)

But if I get a loan from a bank, I'm only putting down $10,000 out-of-pocket and I'm getting $10,000 a year in income. I'm actually getting 100 percent return on the actual cash that was outlaid because the bank is fronting the money. In other words, I'm getting a 100 percent return on my "cash-in."

That's why rental real estate can be such a great option—as long as market prices don't go down dramatically. Even if the market stays stable, without going up, it's a great way to make money. I'm only putting 10 percent of my own money "in" and I'm getting 10 percent "out" (of the home's total value). That equates to a 100 percent return on my actual cash invested. Where else can you get that? Nowhere. The only way you can do it is if you're able to borrow the money—that's the definition of leverage. If the investment goes well, it's a very positive scenario.

However, if the investment doesn't go well, that's when the leverage works and compounds against you, like we saw with Lehman Brothers in 2007. They had borrowed (were leveraged) 45 more times than they actually had in cash.

This is the riskier part of the second approach to rental income. If you become overleveraged, small price fluctuations in your underlying assets (property prices) can mean huge divergences in your financial statement and balance sheet. That's exactly what happened to a large portion of the country, as we found out when the financial crisis hit.

Not even the highly wealthy are immune. Let's say a high-powered mogul named Tanner Schmidt III borrowed $1 billion to buy a swanky Manhattan skyscraper. If the value of that building decreased by just 5 percent, all of a sudden Tanner's net worth changed by $50 million in an instant. Pretty soon we're talking real money, right? Tanner just choked on his monocle. (Don't worry, Tanner—this was just a hypothetical.)

I only point out the risk to make you aware. Borrowing money is still a great way to buy the right real estate and generate rental income—as long as you don't overextend yourself. Make sure you only leverage what you can handle and not a penny more.

What do I mean by "only leverage what you can handle"? For retirees, imagine all of your real estate loans were called at once. Sure, you could sell properties (hopefully in a timely manner) and pay the loans off. But what if you could not? Think about the financial situation that would put you in. All of a sudden banks are demanding their money back, essentially "calling your loan." If you don't have the liquid resources to do so, and if your properties are illiquid, you can quickly become insolvent. So, keep this in mind before you take on *too much* leverage or debt.

Investment Income

In its simplest form, investment income is a combination of the income-generating power of all your accumulated *assets*—cash, stocks, bonds, mutual funds, exchange traded funds (ETFs), REITs, closed-end funds, master limited partnership stocks (MLPs), energy royalty trusts, etc.

Here's the thing you need to know: that combination of assets has to grow over time so that one day, when you stop adding to it, it will do the work for you, generating enough income to supplement all of the other areas that I just described. So how do you put yourself into a position where it can? You spend much of your life building this lump sum by diverting and saving assets in your retirement reservoir; now it is vitally important that those assets use their own momentum to generate both growth (appreciation) and income (cash flow).

While you're working, you should be accumulating wealth inside of your:

- 401(k)
- 403(b)
- 457 plans
- Roth IRAs
- Regular IRAs
- Investment accounts
- Savings accounts

Those are the multiple places you're going to put your money in order to build the aforementioned reservoir. Now let's talk about "growth" versus "income" when it comes to how your savings can grow.

People are very used to thinking about investment money in terms of *growth*, and that's a good thing. The reservoir needs to get bigger. I want to buy stock at $10, and I want it to go up to $11 and then $12, and then eventually up to $20 and beyond. That is the definition of what's called "capital appreciation"—also known as "growth investing."

"But Wes," you might be thinking. "Is there any other way?" Funny you should ask. There are hundreds of different ways to invest, but they all center around the growth of your capital.

Take, for example, an income-oriented approach. Let's say you buy stock for $10, and each year that stock pays a $1 dividend. Over the course of 10 years, you end up with $20. Your original share price didn't change—it stayed at $10—but the company paid a $1 dividend to you each year. (See Illustration 7.1.)

Illustration 7.1 Turning $10 into $20 Using Two Very Different Approaches

All Growth Example	Beginning	Year 1	Year 2	Year 3	Year 4	Year 5	Year 6	Year 7	Year 8	Year 9	Year 10	Total
Stock ABC												
Stock Price	$10	$11	$12	$13	$14	$15	$16	$17	$18	$19	$20	$20
Dividends	0	0	0	0	0	0	0	0	0	0	0	$0
												$20

All Income Example	Beginning	Year 1	Year 2	Year 3	Year 4	Year 5	Year 6	Year 7	Year 8	Year 9	Year 10	Total
Stock XYZ												
Stock Price	$10	$10	$10	$10	$10	$10	$10	$10	$10	$10	$10	$10
Dividends		$1	$1	$1	$1	$1	$1	$1	$1	$1	$1	$10
												$20

In this example, both all-growth and all-income investing get you to the same result—your $10 has become $20—but you get there in very different ways.

You end up with the same amount as you would if, rather than paying a dividend, the stock price grew to $20 per share.

I use this example to explain the difference between *income investing* and *growth investing* to my clients and radio show listeners. Take a look at Illustration 7.1.

In the all-growth example, stock ABC goes up by $1 every year for 10 years—and your original $10, grows to $20. In the all-income example, stock XYZ stays totally level for 10 years and pays you $1 per year. So, you are left with $10 in the original XYZ stock price *plus* $10 in dividends, leaving you with $20. In both cases, you're left with the exact same amount of money. But you have arrived at the same result in very different ways. That, in essence, describes the difference between growth investing and income investing.

Both methodologies can work, but I believe income investing provides more predictability and consistency when structured correctly. Imagine if every single component of your retirement portfolio (every stock, bond, mutual fund, ETF, etc.) paid you some level of consistent predictable cash flow. Think of 20 or 30 or 40 different components all doing some version of what stock XYZ does in Illustration 7.1.

Where do these 20 to 40 different components come from?

The DID Approach to Income Investing: Dividends, Interest, and Distribution

- **Dividends** come from stocks—usually large U.S. and international companies and real estate investment trusts or REITs.
- **Interest** comes from *various* types of bonds—government, municipal, corporate, high yield, floating rate, treasury inflation protected securities (TIPS), and international bonds.

- **Distributions** come from a whole host of other areas, including master limited partnerships (MLPs), closed-end funds (CEFs), and energy royalty trusts.

The key to income investing is to have multiple income-producing components all working for you in a harmonious balance. Using the DID approach allows you to have a highly diversified strategy of generating income and a highly diversified way to allocate your investments so that they are not in one basket or bucket. (I will delve deeper into the "bucket approach" to income investing in Chapter 8.)

Quite simply, the areas I described above add up to a *cash flow*, which is why I want to at least get them on your radar. What they all have in common is that they come to you (or get added to your investment accounts) as new money market funds—essentially cash, as if you had just received a paycheck. **When you are in retirement, this cash income is an essential tributary.**

At times, the cash flow can be as much as you were used to seeing from your W-2 paycheck. Of course, this depends on the size of the reservoir that you've built and your level of percentage yield (aka the level of cash flow that gets produced). One thing I love about this is that you start the year with a portfolio yield—cash flow divided by your overall portfolio value—and the result in actual cash flow is often very predictable. That means at the beginning of each year, if you know your portfolio yield, you will know with a high degree of accuracy how much cash flow your portfolio should generate for the coming year, regardless of how much "markets" go up or down in a given year.

For example: Let's say I get $5,000 in cash flow on $100,000. That means I'm getting a 5 percent cash flow. That means that my portfolio yield is 5 percent. So, if I start the year out with a 5 percent yield, then that part of my portfolio experience is very predictable. The yield and cash flow should generally be the same for the next year (or more), and there's a high level of comfort that comes along with that. A portfolio of $100,000 that has a yield, or cash flow, of 5 percent should produce $5,000 in new cash flow—and that's just the cash flow—regardless of how much the overall portfolio value changes (appreciates or depreciates) in a given year.

- **Good market example.** $100,000 portfolio with 5% yield = $5,000 in cash flow. But the stock market had a good year, so in addition to collecting your $5,000 in cash, the portfolio value may also end the year higher, at $110,000.
- **Bad market example.** $100,000 portfolio with a 5% yield = $5,000 in cash flow. But the stock market had a bad year, so in addition to collecting your $5,000 in cash, the portfolio value may also end the year lower, at $90,000. But that's okay because you've collected your $5,000, and you haven't touched the "principal value" of the portfolio. You have only taken the cash flow and can now wait until the principal value has a chance to rebound in price (which may take time).

The important part to focus on here is separating your portfolio's *cash-producing ability* from its overall ability to grow in value over time.

Yes, we want *both* income and growth—but in any given year only the cash flow part is highly predictable, so it's the only stream we can count on.

The More Streams of Income, the More Freely Happiness Will Flow

Now that I've shown you the various types of income streams you can bring in, let's talk about their correlation to happiness. Specifically, I want to answer a few very important questions.

- What is the amount of income you need?
- How are you going to get that income?
- Is happiness directly related to the number of income streams?

Let's first figure out the amount of income you need. Refer to Illustration 7.2.

The mean, or average, income for the happy group falls right around $82,770 per year, whereas the average income for the unhappy group lands at $55,370. What does this reveal? A lot!

More income equals more happiness—but only to a point. The place where the amount of income needed starts to level off shows yet another example of the "plateau effect." I want you to understand this concept and the average level where it occurs so that you can have an inflection point to shoot for (Illustration 7.3).

Now, for current retirees, what's the magic number to reach in retirement income? I'm looking for an inflection point: the exact point where people begin to jump from "not" and "slightly" happy to "moderately," "very," and "extremely" happy. When I tabulate the data from these graphs, I get $72,277.

Illustration 7.2   Happiness by Current Income (Mean)

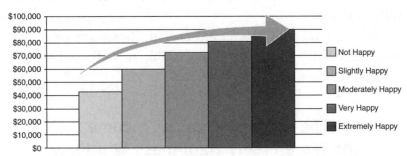

It probably won't surprise you to see that higher income equates to more happiness. But look more closely, and you'll see the plateau effect as happiness levels off.

Illustration 7.3   Peak Annual Earnings for Each Happiness Level

Happiness Level	H5	H4	H3	H2	H1
Peak Annual Earnings	$104,268	$95,795	$85,385	$81,034	$65,300

Happy Group Average	Unhappy Group Average
$97,869	$77,522

This data reflects the "peak income" of people who are within 10 years of retirement or in retirement currently.

1. Assuming a 20 percent tax rate, let's multiply $72,277 by 0.8, which gives us $57,281 per year.
2. Divide that by 12 months, which gives us $4,818 per month. In other words, to reach a sense of moderate happiness, the average retiree needs to have close to $5,000 of spending money per month.

My survey data tell me that a meager 15 percent of the happy group have only one income source. We can deduce it's pretty hard to achieve happiness with only one source, right? You need more than that, obviously—but how many more?

Thirty-five percent of happy retirees have two income sources and 32 percent have three, but there's a steep drop-off with four income sources—it falls all the way to 11 percent. That tells us it's pretty tough to have four income sources. Still, if you can do it, go for it. You're livin' the dream.

If we look at the big picture here, we come up with one key point. The more (and different) income sources you can rely on in retirement, the more income stream diversification you will have. That leads to a higher sense of safety, security, and the cushion that is so important to our sense of well-being and happiness.

The Most Common Income Streams
for the Happiest Retirees

What were the most common sources streaming toward the reservoir? Social security was the number one answer. Some retirees had social security and disability. Some had social security and a pension. Some had social security and investment income.

If you look at the moderately happy to extremely happy group, there are some interesting conclusions. The diversification of streams was higher for this group, which wasn't surprising.

The extremely happy group mostly listed pensions first as their primary source, then dividend income after that. They also listed part-time work mixed with social security. Some other source combinations that came up were corporate pensions, teacher retirement pensions, social security, rental, and portfolio income. These people know how to diversify—and I love it!

These are the income streams many of the happiest people were receiving. I want you to see why it makes so much sense, because I want you to be just as happy as they are. I want you to focus on the importance of diversifying the money you live on. Ideally, I want you to start this at an early age, but the important thing is to start now. I know you can do it because you're smart enough to be reading this book.

No *One* Is Perfect—Plan
and Diversify Accordingly

There is no *one* perfect source of income. Even if you own a $20 million building free and clear that pays you a clean $1 million per year in net cash flow, it could be taken down by an earthquake (worst-case scenario). I'm exaggerating merely to show the importance of diversifying your sources so you can keep standing if one of them takes a hit.

For the Gen X- and Gen Yers reading this book, there's a good chance your social security benefits will be reduced by the time you reach retirement. Don't sulk. It's the way it is, and you need to adapt by having an even higher income. **You also need to sharpen your focus on creating your own income sources.**

If you are a proud member of Gen X (the generation born after the baby boom, between the 1960s and the early 1980s) or a millennial (birth dates in the mid to late 1980s and onward), you need to save even more than your parents and grandparents did. Raise the walls of that reservoir so more water can flow in and you can generate more income through income investments.

Put a greater weight on a 401(k), 403(b), or 457 plan, depending on your specific situation. As a millennial, there will most likely be less financial support from your company and government in your retirement years by the time you get there.

It's not your parents' or grandparents' fault. Don't blame them. The system was built for a certain life expectancy and, put simply, people are living longer today than they used to. If the social security and pension architects had known the generation after my grandfather, who worked at DuPont until he was 64 and died at 74, was going to be full of people living until 85, they would've calculated for it and made the monthly pension payouts smaller.

Be glad your grandpappy and nana are still alive! Extra years of life for your loved ones are a positive thing, and worth the cost of having a little less extra money coming in from some Fortune 500 company. Sure, more of the onus is on you to provide for yourself, but that's okay because you're reading this book. You're smart and resourceful. You're the future. You'll be able to retire sooner than you think!

I want you to find comfort as you head toward retirement, and one way to do that is by observing money secret #4: combining several different tributaries to form one significant income stream. Develop an income stream of three or four sources, not just one, and put yourself in the position to retire happy. Before long, you'll be floating on top of your own financial reservoir, mai tai in hand, without a care in the world.

Three Tips on Generating Multiple Income Streams

1. Find (and purchase) several properties (homes or buildings) that produce rent.
2. Decide the best time to begin taking your social security payments. In 2012, social security payments averaged around $1,200 a month. But, payments could be more than $3,000 for some recipients—depending on age, date you begin payments, and previous income.[4]
3. Achieve a certain level of reliable, safe, and predictable investment income (more on this in the next chapter).

If you're reading this book long before the typical retirement age, I want you to consider putting a heavier weight on your job path—or job paths, if you have more than one. Is a pension available? Many of our nation's teachers have pension plans. The state of Georgia has a great one. California, Michigan, and Pennsylvania have their own versions too. These are what I would consider healthy pension programs. Same goes for some of the civil service jobs—government positions, police officers, firefighters. These are jobs that still have significant pension plans. If you work one of these jobs and don't have a pension set up, you should!

If you're closer to retirement, I want you to focus on ways to diversify while staying active. I want you to look into working part-time. Find a way to allow several income sources to trickle in so that if one tributary runs dry, there are several others still flowing that can pay the bills.

CHAPTER 8

Secret #5

Become an Income Investor

open every radio show by telling my listeners there are a lot of ways to invest. Countless people have invented countless manners, methods, and philosophies about how to make money in the market.

There's growth investing, value investing, GARP investing (Growth At a Reasonable Price), global macro, sector rotation strategies, merger arbitrage, and long/short credit. You can invest in specialty areas like oil, soft commodities, and gold-oriented investments. There are bottom up investors, top down investors, and everything in between.

So then, with so many possibilities beckoning you and your money, why do I believe so strongly in income investing? It's a great question.

Do I believe income investing is the only way to get the most out of your money? This kind of dramatic question usually provides the perfect cliffhanger for me to go to a commercial break. But since we're not on the radio, I'll cut to the chase and give you the answer.

No, I don't believe that.

Income investing is not the only way. It's not the be-all and end-all of handling your financial situation. There is no magic formula for everything (or for anything, frankly).

And yet despite the fact that there are no magic formulas, I still point the people I work with firmly in this direction. Income investing is the method I've used and developed over the course of many years, and the one I find brings a lot of comfort and certainty to an otherwise uncertain practice.

Not every football team uses the same offense to win games. Not every coach draws the same Xs and Os on his chalkboard. But when you find that coach who knows how to craft and teach his knowledge in a way that maximizes the talent around him, that's when teams start winning championships.

In this chapter, I'm going to give you the rundown on income investing so you can decide if it's right for you. Consider income investing your game plan and me your coach. Let's put our team on the field and go win us some games.

What Is Income Investing?

It's really pretty simple. **Income investing is a way to generate consistent cash flow from your liquid investments.** It comes from three places:

1. Dividends from stocks
2. Interest from various types of bonds
3. Distributions that come from a variety of investments—investments that pay distributions but don't fit neatly in the stock or bond category

So cash flow is generated from dividends, interest, and distributions. Add those three together and you have your *personal portfolio yield.*

Yield is a function of how much cash flow you're getting in relation to the assets you have invested. So, what is your annual cash flow?[1] Let's say you start the year out with a yield of 3.5 or 4 percent and know with a great degree of certainty—though nothing is guaranteed—that you're going to generate that 4 percent in cash flow from your investments.

That 4 percent, whether it's on $240,000, $480,000, $720,000, or any other amount, is the predictable part of the portfolio. That's the slice of the pie you can rely on. Isn't it nice to have something predictable in an otherwise uncertain world?

Remember: income investing focuses on the production of steady cash flow from dividends, interest, and distributions which can either be reinvested in your portfolio or used to fund your spending needs. This differs from pure growth investing that relies on a rising stock market alone. For a refresher on the difference between income investing and growth investing revisit Chapter 7.

How Do You Become an Income Investor?

When most people think of their investment account—most commonly a 401(k) plan—they imagine their assets inside a pie chart. They see green, blue, yellow, red, big, small, large, international, domestic, emerging markets, specialty areas, commodities, and gold all crammed into one pie chart that is supposed to make investing, from a visual perspective, easy to understand.

I've been in the investment industry for a long time, and for the most part, I have no problem with pie charts. However, the time I've spent hosting *Money Matters* has helped me understand the following: nobody has time for complex graphs and ideas.

Generally speaking, the simpler the explanation of an investment philosophy, the more buy-in it will get. Because I believe so strongly in income investing, I am continually refining and simplifying the way I describe it to people.

I've had to come up with a way for both clients and radio listeners to understand my investment process and philosophy, just by talking to them over the air, on the phone, and when I sit down in meetings.

So instead of using that pie chart, I've developed the Wes Moss Bucket System. When conducting a meeting with a new investor who isn't familiar with the terminology "income investing," I take him or her through a series of bucket diagrams to explain the process. Now I'm going to do the same for you.

Introducing the Wes Moss Bucket System

The buckets in my system don't include physical real estate such as land or homes, and they don't include private business ownership. They only refer to money you could invest in a traditional investment portfolio. It's all very liquid, which is why I chose buckets. Clever, right? I thought so.

The bucket drawings I'll share in this chapter are simply an attempt to give you a visualization of the mechanics or blueprints of what's actually happening inside your portfolio—Roth IRA, 401(k), 403(b)—or any sort of account where you are investing money.

Look at Illustration 8.1 and you'll see the four buckets. The title of each bucket is its focus.

1. Cash bucket
2. Income bucket
3. Growth bucket
4. Alternative income bucket

Illustration 8.1   Beginning Buckets, Overview

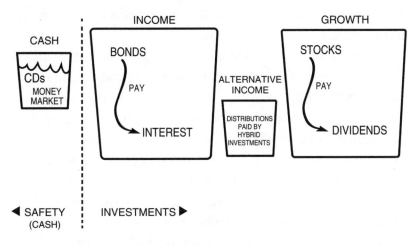

These are the only four places your liquid money can go.

I've drawn a dotted line between cash and income. To the left of this dotted line is where your safe money goes. To the right of this line is where your investable dollars go.

The left side of this line, that's safe money. That's cash, or what I also refer to as your emergency cash. Having this cash on hand helps you sleep at night, knowing you can quickly cover an emergency expense if it comes up. What's in the *cash bucket*? CDs and money markets.

You'll notice the bucket looks to be filled with water. This is meant to reflect the amount of liquid money you have to provide for you and your family for six months of financial hardship. That amount will differ for each person. It might be $30,000, $60,000, $100,000, or some other number. Whatever six months of money means for you is the amount of money in that bucket of CDs and money markets.

The right side of the dotted line reflects that you're investing those "investable dollars" so you can outpace inflation, maintain purchasing power of your money, and allow your money to work for you over time. That's why these are investments and not savings. In fact, that's the difference between investments and savings.

Primarily what you'll find inside the *income bucket* are various sorts of bonds, which is why it can also be referred to as the bond bucket. Within this space are government bonds that have yields from 0 to 3 or 4 percent, corporate bonds that pay 2 to 4.5 percent, and high-yield bonds that pay 4.5 to 7.5 or 8 percent. That's the yield I talked about earlier in the chapter. The yield represents the level of interest being paid on a bond. Bonds pay interest.

The *growth bucket* is going to be full of various kinds of stocks. It is essentially your stock bucket—small cap, mid cap, and large cap stocks. For the purposes of this book, we'll focus on two types of stocks in general: dividend stocks and growth stocks.

The *alternative income bucket* is where you find hybrid investments—not traditional bonds or stocks, but all the areas that lie in between.

Still with me? Good.

Take a look at Illustration 8.2. In the income bucket, you'll find a number of different types of bonds.

- Government and municipal bonds
- Corporate bonds
- High-yield bonds

Government bonds equate to government Treasuries, short-term Treasury bills, and intermediate and long-term government bonds. Also included here are Treasury inflation-protected securities—TIPS. Municipal bonds are issued by state and local governments and typically offer income that is exempt from federal taxes (and state taxes if you live in the state where they are issued). Like all of these major bond categories, municipal bonds are issued with various maturities (how many years they pay interest) and various credit ratings that measure the issuers' creditworthiness.

Illustration 8.2   The Income Bucket

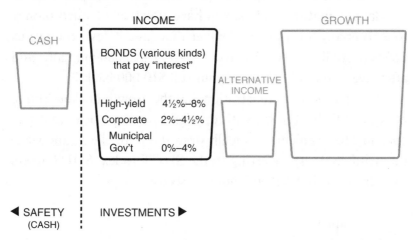

Here's a closer look at the income bucket.

Corporate bonds become available from large corporations such as Apple or Ford Motor Company when they need to fund large projects. These are companies that will likely be around for many years to come, which makes them dependable.

Then you get to the next category, high-yield bonds, which is a fancy and nice word for junk bonds. Junk bonds pay higher interest—4.5 to 8 percent per year—because they're not as stable. They're like people with bad credit—they have to pay a higher interest rate to borrow money.

Bonds are basically IOUs because you are essentially loaning money to the government or company, whereas with stocks you actually own a portion of the company. Hence the phrase: "loan vs. own."

As I said, with bonds you're a lender to a company or a government because they need your money to do a specific project. You lend them money for a specific amount of time—3 years, 10 years, etc.—and then they give you a coupon or set interest payment every year over the life of that bond.

When the term is up, they pay you your principal back on the date of maturity. Thus, you have effectively loaned money to a company for a piece of paper that says, "Hey, you give us $10,000, we'll give you 5 percent on that $10,000 annually, and after five years we'll give you your full $10,000 back."

Now let's look at Illustration 8.3: the growth bucket. You're going to fill this bucket with dividend-paying stocks that pay around 2 to 5 percent. I typically draw it out for clients and write the word "SHUT," referring to the SHUT Index. SHUT refers to four of the 10 S&P 500 industry sectors:

- Staples
- Healthcare
- Utilities
- Telecommunications

Staple companies are those like Coca-Cola, Clorox, and Procter & Gamble. Examples of healthcare companies are Bristol-Myers Squibb, Eli Lilly, and Pfizer. For utility companies, think

Illustration 8.3   The Growth Bucket

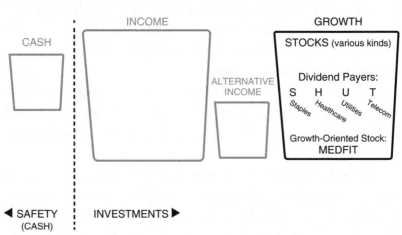

Here's a closer look at the growth bucket.

Southern Company, Consolidated Edison, and Duke Energy. For telecom, look at names like AT&T and Verizon, among others.

These are companies that pay dividends of about 2 percent up to about 5 percent—and sometimes even more than that. Here we are dealing with noncyclical industries. And by and large, the SHUT index is composed of dividend-paying stocks.

For the other six industries, I use the MEDFIT acronym—materials, energy, discretionary, financials, industrial companies, and technology. By and large, these sectors tend to lean toward growth companies (not to say they are totally devoid of some fantastic dividend-payers).

Now look at Illustration 8.4. This is a good time to explain a bit more about what goes into the alternative income bucket. Anything that doesn't fit neatly into the other categories goes here. For instance, pipeline and energy storage companies would go here. MLPs (master limited partnerships) make up a large portion of these companies. Due to their legal structure, MLPs pay nearly all of their net profits back out to shareholders in the form of distributions.

Illustration 8.4   The Alternative Income Bucket

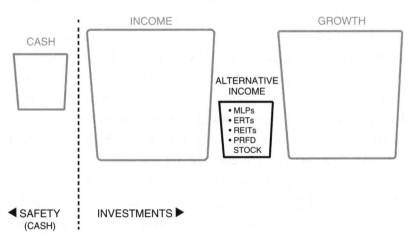

Here's a closer look at the alternative income bucket.

That's why we see yields in the 4 to 7 percent range. An example would be the largest pipeline company in America—Enterprise Products Partners, LP. EPD has many thousands of miles of pipeline that run from the Gulf of Mexico to Wisconsin to New York, and from North Carolina to Wyoming.

Another type that fits in the alternative bucket are ERTs—energy royalty trusts. These are crude oil and natural gas trusts that are technically land trusts with oil wells and gas wells sitting on top of them. Similar to MLPs, ERTs have a legal structure that requires a nearly 100 percent pass-through royalty payout to investors. That royalty is based on the value and the price of the commodity (i.e., is oil at $80? $90? $100 per barrel?) and the amount of production they are able to pull out of the ground during any given quarter. They pass a percentage of that royalty on to you. ERTs will typically have yields between 5 and 10 percent per year.

If you're enjoying all the acronyms in the alternative income bucket, you're in luck! I have another one for you—REIT. It stands for real estate investment trust. These are typically commercial, publicly traded companies. They include big apartment companies like Post Properties here in Atlanta and Simon Property Group out of Indianapolis.

A great example of an REIT scenario would be an individual store such as Cartier Jewelers, J.Crew, or Cinnabon leasing space from Simon. They pay on that lease to Simon, who makes a profit and then distributes that profit to you as a unit holder. The legal structure of REITs requires roughly 90 percent of the net profits to go back out to shareholders. You'll see REITs paying anywhere from a 3 to 5 percent dividend and above.

Needless to say, this alternative bucket is quite interesting. It's like the teenage offspring of the other buckets. Sure, it got its nose pierced in high school, but that's okay because it still made the honor roll a few semesters. This is the bucket where you will typically find the highest percentage annual yielders.

Okay, so we've now covered the main examples of the core investments that go in each bucket—cash, income, growth, and alternative income. Now let's look at all the buckets and their approximate yields (Illustration 8.5).

Depending on what type of bonds you own, the income bucket should pay anywhere from a 0 to 8 percent yield. The 0 percent would most likely be on ultra short-term government bonds, and the 8 percent would be the highest-risk junk bonds.

High-yield bonds (junk bonds) pay a high yield because they are on the high end of the risk ladder. You know that top rung of the ladder you're not supposed to stand on? Some junk bonds are basically that top step. A few steps down from there near the middle of the ladder are corporate bonds. You'll see low-risk, low-yield bonds at the bottom of the yield ladder with government bonds.

If you were to structure the income part of your portfolio with various kinds of bonds, referred to in fancy Wall Street lingo as *fixed income*, you're going to have a yield somewhere between 0 and 8 percent. So, a fully diversified bond portfolio

Illustration 8.5   All Buckets with Approximate Yield

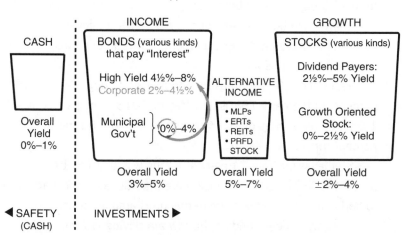

Here you'll see each bucket with its approximate overall yield beneath it.

should have a yield of somewhere between 3 and 5 percent at today's prevailing rates.

Why Would You Put Money into a "0 Percent" Government Bond?

For total and complete safety! Very short-term government bonds known as Treasury bills or Treasury notes can mature in as little as 30 days or up to 10 years.

The interest that you will receive on short-term government bonds will be from a fraction of a percent up to approximately 3 percent as of 2014.

So for the most part "zero" is a slight understatement, as one-year notes pay about 0.1 percent, while seven-year notes pay about 2 percent—so you are actually making *some* interest. Second, it's even safer than a regular savings account because if you are a large investor putting $20 million in a savings account, only $250,000 of that will be insured by the FDIC.

Therefore these low-yield bonds are another way to have extremely safe money that's only tied up for a very short term—30-day Treasury bills, etc.

There have been times when very short-term government bonds have paid 1 or 2 percent, but it all depends on where interest rates are.

Years ago, 10-year Treasury bonds used to pay 14 percent (in the early 1980s). In May of 2013, they paid 1.6 percent—and as of 2014 were hovering around the 3 percent range.

So they went from 14 percent all the way down to 1.6 percent (1980 to 2013). It took more than 30 years for that to happen, but this shows the tremendous amount of change.

So, government bonds right now are paying *virtually* zero percent on many short-term maturities, only because we are

in a very low-interest-rate environment. It's not normal for
rates to be at this level, and it is occurring only because the
Federal Reserve is forcing interest rates to be low in order
to stimulate the economy. Low interest rates mean cheaper
loans, cheaper mortgages, and cheaper car notes—and
often stir consumer activity and spending.

Look at Illustration 8.5 again. The income bucket should
pay you around 3 to 5 percent, the growth bucket should pay you
between 2 and 4 percent, the alternative income bucket should
pay you between 5 and 7 percent, and your cash right now should
pay you 0 to 1 percent.

Now it's all about connecting pipelines. All of the buckets,
to some extent, are interconnected. The pipelines are there to
transport the income that will be generated from the investments
in each bucket. At some point these pipelines are going to serve a
purpose, because the money or income that is generated is going
to come back to you (Illustration 8.6).

Why are money markets paying such a low rate of interest? Wasn't there a time when you could get 4 to 5 percent in
CDs? Absolutely! These short-term rates are effectively set and
controlled by the Federal Reserve, which is now headed up by
Janet Yellen. When Janet and her team set the federal funds rate
between 0 and 0.25 percent, that means banks can't really pay
you much more than that without losing money.

To review: we keep our safe money to the left in the emergency or cash bucket, we keep our investments to the right in
the growth, income, and alternative income buckets. Each of
the three buckets on the right pays a consistent level of income—
3 to 5 percent, 5 to 7 percent, and 2 to 4 percent.

It's worth mentioning that bonds are different animals than
stocks, which are different animals than the alternative hybrid
group. So by nature, instead of a typical pie chart dividing up

Illustration 8.6   The Cash Flow Generating Bucket System at Work

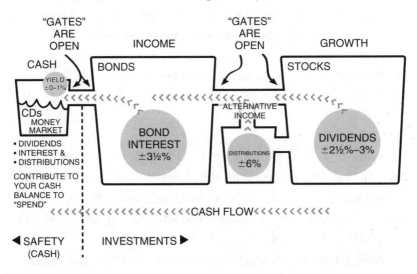

Now your investment buckets are *all* producing income (cash flow) that consistently adds to your cash bucket, which is *portfolio income* you can *spend.*

Look at that money flow!

your money, I'm literally showing you how it's divided up into four separate areas that all have their own set of characteristics and all serve their own purpose.

They all do something slightly different. But they all are there to increase your wealth and preserve and grow your capital in some way, shape, or form over time.

The Balance of the Buckets

I am an enormous believer in what I call the balance of the buckets. Sounds epic, right? We'll talk about the different percentages of what to put in the buckets in the next chapter, but to me there's a lot of power in getting this step right to begin with.

The number one most important thing you can do as an investor is understand this bucket system before you invest another penny. I want you to understand how your investments fall into these very separate and critically important areas of the world.

So I've put your money into four areas, and each one gives you a yield. Let's target a specific yield. Income's going to give you 4 percent. Growth is going to give you 3 percent, and alternative income is going to give you 6 percent. That means you have an overall portfolio yield of around 4 percent . . . in today's world.

As an example, let's say you have 40 percent in income, 10 percent in alternative income, and 50 percent in growth. Thus, you have 40 percent in the bond bucket and 60 percent in the alternative and growth bucket. That would equate to a yield of about 4 percent overall, in 2014. That figure could be 4.5 percent or 5 percent in 2015 and 5 or 5.5 percent in 2016, but as of the time of writing, you can count on around 4 percent in yield in today's environment.

That, in my opinion, should be on the low end of the historic continuum. In fact, the cash flow you get from income investing over the next several years may grow because interest rates will likely rise over the next several years. Hence, the income bucket/ bond bucket might pay you a little more than it's paying today. But using a conservative estimate, this is what your income could look like.

So back to my example: whether you have $240,000 or $2.5 million, you should be able to generate a steady cash flow of 4 percent from that number.

What If You Don't Need the Income Right Now?

Let me talk for a minute about the accumulation phase. Let's assume you are in your thirties, forties, or fifties. All your interest from that income bucket is generated from your bonds, and it just stays in the bucket. Visualize that income hitting the wall of your bucket and coming back in to buy more bonds. The money keeps being reinvested and reinvested over a long period of time.

You do the same thing with the growth bucket. You have a dividend paid to you from your stocks, it hits the wall of the growth bucket and *is reinvested*. And again, the reinvestment of those dividends and the interest and distributions—that's all part of what makes your money grow over time.

It's important to note the fact that all of the pipeline "gates" in this bucket diagram are shut. There's no money flowing from one bucket to another right now. What do you do with all of that income? Reinvest. And reinvest. And reinvest. Now you are really accumulating! See Illustration 8.7.

Look at Illustration 8.6 one final time. I want you to imagine all your buckets are fully functioning and you're heading toward

Illustration 8.7 All Buckets with Approximate Yield, and "Gates Closed"

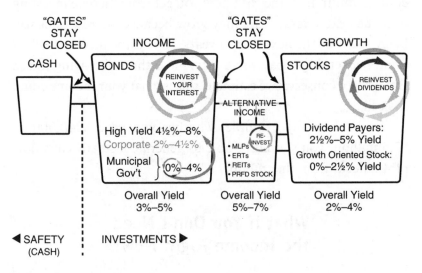

Buckets if you **don't need** the income/cash flow today

This diagram shows all the buckets with approximate yield and the pipeline "gates closed" with the reinvestment feature in full effect.

the end zone. You're in retirement. Like Elvis, the accumulation phase has left the building.

You're in the distribution phase now, which means you get to spend some of that money! All those years you spent in the office kitchen singing "Happy Birthday" to coworkers you hardly knew are about to pay off.

This step is generally for people between the ages of 60 and 100. The only thing that happens here is that now the pipelines are open. The growth bucket pipeline is open. The alternative income bucket pipeline is open. The income valves are open. All of a sudden, the cash flow that you're generating is no longer being reinvested anywhere but rather ending up in your wallet.

It's flowing back into the cash bucket—the one all the way to the left. It's coming back to you to solve the biggest fear in the world: not having a paycheck. Well, guess what? You created your own paycheck. You're an income producing monster. Congratulations!

All those dividends, all that interest, all those distributions: they now flow back into that nice, easy-looking cash bucket. All your buckets are producing money for you in excess of your emergency fund that you can use to live on. You have income, and you have cash flow each month, just like when you were working.

A quick note: In today's economic climate (and with low interest rates), it's a tall task to get the full 5 percent just in income that I typically like to see from a portfolio. But, remember, we still haven't accounted for *growth* and *appreciation*, which should also, over time, add to the portfolio's overall return—largely from the alternative bucket and the growth bucket.

Even though you might only be *yielding* 4 percent in a given year, if the stock market in general does well, the energy market does well, the pipeline companies do well, and REITs do well, then over time you're also going to get some appreciation out of the last two buckets. So if those are growing at 5 and 6 and 7 and 8 percent per year, then it makes sense to expect your *4 percent in income* and then see another few percentage points of appreciation on top of that in a decent market.

A Quick Note About Gold

If you watch certain news channels, you've no doubt been inundated with commercials urging you to invest in gold. What do I think about gold? Not a big fan. I don't mind if you want to invest in small amounts, but really, gold investing is the opposite of income investing.

Gold investments don't really give you anything. In fact, Warren Buffet famously wrote about how he'd rather own all the farmland in the Midwestern United States than all the gold in the world.[2] Why? Not only does gold not pay a dividend, it actually costs money to store—so there's a heavy carrying cost associated with owning it. Think about farmland. It produces crops that yield cash. If you grow more crops, you get more cash. Furthermore, farmland in America is producing something usable.

So, if you're stuck on gold, go ahead and invest a little, but remember that Warren and I are against it.

The Bucket System Isn't the *Only* Way— But It's a Great Place to Start

My bucket system takes the very complex world of investing and simplifies it by helping you visualize your investments as money dropped into one of four easy-to-understand "buckets." Over the years, I've found this to be the most effective way of explaining income investing to the families I work with every day.

Remember: income investing is *a* philosophy, not the *only* philosophy. However, it's a philosophy that I am very passionate about. It's not an 80-yard pass down the field for a touchdown. Rather, it's a solid game plan of 5- and 6-yard runs that gets you a first down most of the time.

It's one of the few ways I know to easily understand what your money is doing for you and how to be realistic on a systematic basis. Income investing is not a magic bullet. It's a system that works over time. The system itself may not be sexy, but the results you'll achieve are runway model quality.

The next time someone promises you a "never lose" financial scheme, remember that even if there is such a thing as a free lunch, you'll still get stuck paying for parking and eating rubber chicken. **With my bucket system, you at least have control over a big part of the process—and that's the income part.** It's not a free lunch, but at least you'll know what's on the menu.

The bucket system can be a true hedge against inflation, and I encourage you to try thinking about your current investments using the bucket system as your focus. Income investing is not just for "old people." It's for anyone looking for a predictable path to earning money over time. **If you don't need the income, reinvest it! If you do need the income, open the valves and start taking the money.** Your hard work and disciplined planning will allow your portfolio to become the working stiff you used to be.

In the next two chapters, I'll go into income investing in greater depth, sharing the toolkit of tips, tricks, and strategies that make me such a fan of this philosophy. When we're done, you'll be able to decide if income investing is right for you.

Four Easy Buckets: Reviewing the Wes Moss Bucket System

I've thrown a lot of valuable information your way, so let's do a quick recap of the four buckets and what they mean for you:

1. **Cash bucket.** This is the money you invest in FDIC-insured accounts. The principal is 100 percent secure but earns very little interest—currently about 1 percent (or less). This money is your most stable and liquid asset. It includes your emergency fund and any extra cash you may need in the next year or two for various purposes.

2. **Income bucket.** Contributions to this bucket are invested in various types of bonds—Treasury, corporate, municipal, high-yield, TIPS, international, and floating rate. They will provide you with interest income. A well-diversified bond portfolio should protect your principal, as well. Diversification within this bucket is especially important for maximizing your return over time.

3. **Growth bucket.** This is the money you have invested in stocks. Your decisions in this area will depend, in part, on your stage of life. If you are in the "accumulation stage"— 25 to 55 or 60 and still working—you should consider owning some growth stocks: shares in companies that have tremendous growth rates but usually don't pay much of a dividend. Their focus is on capital appreciation through growth in their earnings.

   Retirees may want to focus more on dividend-paying stocks. These are companies that aim to give you some capital appreciation and pay you a nice dividend along the way. Dividends accounted for 44 percent of the total

return of the S&P 500 over the last 80 years—part of
the reason I'm such a huge believer in income investing.

4. **Alternative income bucket.** This is for any investment
   that doesn't neatly fit into the income or growth bucket:
   for example, energy royalty trusts (publicly traded oil and
   gas trusts) and MLP stocks (pipeline and energy storage
   companies) that trade just like normal stocks on the NYSE
   (New York Stock Exchange) or other major U.S. indices but
   don't pay traditional dividends or interest. In this example,
   these companies pay out a "distribution."

PART THREE

Minimizing Risk in Your Investment Portfolio

CHAPTER 9

How Risky Can You Be?

Come Up with the Right Mix of Stocks, Bonds, Real Estate, and Cash

One of my favorite investment books is *The Single Best Investment*, by Lowell Miller.[1] In it, he uses the term *bouncing principal* to describe the notion that a steady yield makes it acceptable for your principal to rise and fall (aka bounce) within a reasonable limit. He argues that being a successful investor isn't about playing the market; it's about being a partner in the enterprise and beyond.

In fact, says Lowell, it's really about a "compounding machine that sits quietly off in the corner working for you while you go about your business. It's about harnessing the true power of time and growth, the incredible accumulation of modest gains into enormous ones which is the essence of compounding."

Compounding, Lowell aptly points out, "is the money that money makes, added to the money that money has already made. And each time money makes money, it becomes capable of making even more money than it could before!"

I couldn't agree more. In this chapter, I'll use this kind of mindset to show you how risky you should or shouldn't be in the quest to have your money make money, so it can be added to the money that your money has already made. Let's get to work finding the right mix of stocks, bonds, real estate, and cash so you can retire early and happy.

The Evolution of "Own Your Age in Bonds"

John Bogle is one of my favorite investors of all time. Born in 1929, Bogle is founder of The Vanguard Group, Inc. and president of Vanguard's Bogle Financial Markets Research Center.

For years, Bogle had a rule of thumb to own your age in bonds. People tend to love it. It's very simple, easy to remember, and it worked, so it has been ingrained in the minds of Americans for the last 20 years.

You're 40 years old? Own 40 percent in bonds. Fifty? You know what to do.

It worked by slowly migrating you away from the riskiest part of your portfolio: stocks (i.e., the growth bucket). Thus, as you got closer to needing to use your money, you had less exposure to a big stock market crash or bear market stock correction.

The fact that bonds have provided a very respectable rate of return for the last three decades has made the "own your age in bonds" methodology a very smooth ride. Very simply, bonds have functioned as lower-risk, moderate return investments.

So, for much of this time, Bogle's theory has been a memorable and useful way to think about your portfolio.

Take a look at the interest rate on the 10-year Treasury bond over the last 53 years (Illustration 9.1).

Illustration 9.1   10-Year Treasury Yield Chart 1960–2013

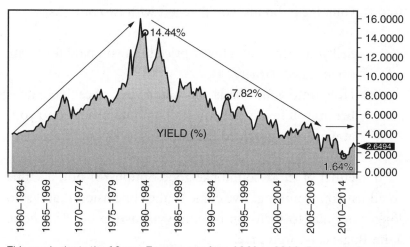

This graph charts the 10-year Treasury rate from 1960 to 2013. Rates rose from the 1960s to 1980 (14 percent) and fell from 1980 to the present. Now interest rates are moving sideways to higher.

As you can see in this chart, interest rates tend to move in long cycles. At this point in time, we've been in a three-decade cycle of steadily descending rates. In general (for the last 30-plus years), they've moved down, then sideways, then down, then sideways. It seems likely that in the next decade we're in for the opposite kind of movement—interest rates moving sideways and up.

So the gusty tailwind that made "own your age in bonds" work for so many different reasons now feels more like a slight breeze at best, and maybe even a slight breeze in your face rather than at your back.

Let's say you buy a 10-year Treasury bond today at 2.5 percent. In two years, the U.S. government might have to pay up to 4 percent to borrow money for 10 years. But it doesn't matter: you're still stuck with that meager 2.5 percent bond for the next eight years. The price of your bond will fall on paper to reflect that today's new higher rates (4 percent) make its 2.5 percent rate from 2 years ago look less attractive to investors. That's true for most bonds in a rising interest rate environment.

If a rising rate environment does happen, and you still want to own your age in bonds, you'll be left with two options:

1. Sell your bonds at a lower price than you paid for them (mentioned earlier).
2. Hold onto your bonds and watch your price fluctuate before you finally get your full amount returned to you at maturity (provided the bond issuer doesn't default).

Do either of those sound like good options? If not, it's time to adjust your thinking. I've come to the conclusion that it's no longer optimal to focus on owning your age in bonds. I hope John Bogle can forgive me!

Adjusting the Bogle: Own Your Age in Income

We all know there are many different ways to invest money. So what is the main reason we choose to hold bonds? For consistent income, right? It's called interest—that's what comes from bonds. It's a simple, predictable piece of your portfolio that doesn't have a lot of downside or risk.

If interest rates rise for the next 30 years and you still want to generate some sort of steady income while trying to maintain your principal, you'll have to do something differently. You know that income comes from a lot of different places, not just bonds. So let's have your new rule of thumb for the next couple of decades be "own your age in income."

Income Clarifier

1. Remember not to confuse the word "income" with the "income bucket" of your portfolio.

2. When I say, "own your age in income," I am referring to any investment that pays you an income. Again, that includes bonds that pay interest, stocks that pay dividends, and alternative investments such as MLPs (energy pipeline stocks) that pay you distributions.

3. So when you're 60 years old, at least 60 percent of the securities you own should be paying you some sort of *income*.

Here's a quick caveat. As an income investor, I'm actually a believer that 90 to 100 percent of what you own should pay you an income, regardless of your age. This is how strongly I feel about income investing as a way to grow (i.e., not run out of) capital over time.

Most of the stocks you could potentially own could pay you some income, but there are companies such as Google that currently offer only pure growth as a means of return—there is no dividend. They don't pay any cash flow directly back to shareholders. I'm not against that kind of investment; it's fine as long as the stocks go up. It's just a different way to invest from the way I teach and practice.

The 10-Year Treasury Rate

The 10-year Treasury rate is an important benchmark because nearly all of the nation's borrowing rates are derived from this interest rate. In other words, wherever the 10-year Treasury rate lands, so goes the average mortgage rate, and so on.

The 10-year Treasury rate is also important because of people's penchant for the safety of buying Treasury bonds.

What's important here is finding the best rate to watch so that you can plan accordingly. This doesn't always prove easy. Legendary economist John Kenneth Galbraith once stated: "The only function of economic forecasting is to make astrology look respectable."

It's a funny line because it contains a kernel of truth. Yet, some economic indicators are actually so reliable, and some patterns so established, that they *can* predict exactly what's going to happen. Not convinced? Let's look at some examples.

If oil prices rise from $80 to $90 a barrel, then gas prices are nearly *certain* to go up within a week or two. Most people only pay attention to the price of a tank of gas—not to its precursor. But West Texas Intermediate, a grade of crude oil used as a benchmark in oil pricing, is a reliable indicator of what you'll pay at the pump.

The same goes for the mortgage market and the interest rate on the 10-year Treasury bonds. As oil is to gas, 10-year Treasury rates are to mortgage rates.

I've been studying the 10-year Treasury bond and its effect on markets since I started in the investment business. In early May 2013, the yield was 1.6 percent. So, if you were to buy a new bond at that level you would be paid 1.6 percent on your money each year for 10 years. At the end of 10 years, the government would pay you back your full principal.

By the end of May 2013, that rate had risen to more than 2.1 percent. That's a full half percent. That may not seem like a lot, but it's a 32 percent rise in interest rates in just a couple of weeks.

The reason? The Federal Reserve (the central bank for the entire U.S. banking system and economy) had begun to *hint* at slowing the monthly rate of their Treasury bond purchases (known as quantitative easing), including the 10-year Treasury bond.

Since the financial crisis, the Fed has done everything in its power to keep interest rates as low as possible. That has allowed rates on government bonds like the 10-year Treasury to drop well under 2 percent. (A rate of 4 percent is probably closer to normal at this point in time.) The Fed's action has dropped mortgage rates to historic lows.

When the Fed lowers short-term rates, it ultimately leads the yield on the 10-year Treasury bond to drop. That causes mortgage rates to drop. You don't have to be Alexander Hamilton to figure that out—it's Economics 101. In April of 2012, the average 30-year mortgage was about 4 percent. Because rates (in 2013) stayed persistently low, the average 30-year mortgage a year later was under 3.5 percent!

Now, because the economy and the job and housing markets have recovered to some extent, the Fed may begin to slow down all the measures it has taken to keep rates low.

In May of 2013, rates on the 10-year Treasury shot up. Predictably, mortgage rates have already started following suit. As of March 31, 2014, the average 30-year mortgage stood at nearly 4.4 percent. That upward trend will likely continue.

Because mortgage rates have bounced back up to the 4 (plus) percent level, applications to refinance mortgages have already begun to drop. So, this may prove the end of the lowest mortgage rates in history. If you haven't already refinanced an existing mortgage, the window may be closing on the balcony of the house you won't get to own.

If you haven't already bought a house, there may still be time to get a mortgage rate in the low 4 percent range—but don't expect that opportunity to last forever.

Thinking of doing a refi? Don't delay. Thinking of buying a home? Start shopping soon. All good things come to an end, and the incredibly low mortgage rates of 2013 and 2014 may soon be nothing but a distant memory.

The Legacy of Inflation: What It Means for You

Look again at Illustration 9.1. The chart shows us that from 1960 to the present, the 10-year Treasury rate started around 4 percent, and then it rose to 5, and then it was at 6, and it slowly continued up, then sideways, then up, then sideways, until at one point in 1981, the 10-year Treasury yield was 14 percent! This meant that if you bought a bond from the U.S. government, that bond paid you 14 percent a year. Cha-ching!

Why was it so high?

The reason was because we also had inflation at double-digit rates. Even though you might've been making 14 percent, if inflation was 10 percent during that short period of time, your real rate of return was only 4 percent. Less enthusiastic cha-ching . . .

You always have to factor in inflation when considering anything you do, but it's even more critical with bonds because inflation is typically 1 to 3 percent and bonds usually pay 3 to 5 percent. Therefore, bonds—particularly government ones—typically only have a small amount of return in excess of inflation, while stocks have historically exceeded inflation fairly significantly.

In general, inflation's a killer of everything. It just takes away your return no matter how you try to make money.

For the most part, from 1960 to 1981, interest rates rose and rose and rose and rose. If you were in the bond market during that time, you could buy bonds each year that paid more in interest than the bond you bought the year before.

Because of the inverse relationship between interest rates and bond price, this made for a tough environment (Illustration 9.2). If you bought a bond that yielded you 6 percent over 5 years and the following year that interest rate went up to 7 percent, buyers would be reluctant to pay you face value for your bond. If you did want to sell your 6 percent bond, most likely you'd have to sell it at a discount. We'll talk more about this later.

Bond investors saw a lot of the same seesaw movement during this era. Interest rates kept going up and up and up, peaking at more than 15 percent in September of 1981. Since then, they've fallen fairly consistently over the last 30 plus years.

Illustration 9.2   Bond Seesaw: The Inverse Relationship of Bonds and Interest Rates

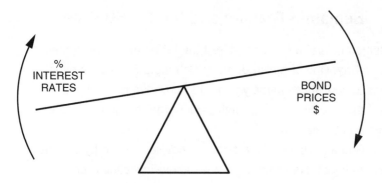

You could make out really well or be ruined financially—it all depends on which side of the seesaw you're sitting on.

So the 10-year Treasury rate went from Mt. Everest in 1981 all the way down to the bottom of the ocean—1.6 percent—as of May 2013.[2] Because of the inverse relationship bond prices have with interest rates, the last three decades have been good for the bond market. Primarily, they've done two things:

1. Paid you a nice interest rate
2. Maintained a price bias to the upside

In other words, bonds have had a tailwind for approximately 32 years because of the bond price to interest rate seesaw relationship. If you've been participating, not only have you gotten a coupon of 3, 4, or 5 percent on the bonds you hold, but if you held individual bonds, bonds ETFs, or bond mutual funds, you very likely saw some price appreciation as well.

Bonds have been an easy and wonderful place to invest (particularly from 1980 until early 2013) with relatively high, steady overall returns (from both income and appreciation) with much less volatility than the stock market.

Benjamin Graham and the 50-50 Rule

Benjamin Graham is considered the father of value-oriented investing. One of his students at Columbia Business School was a man whose name you might know: Warren Buffett. Buffett held him in such high esteem that his son's middle name is Graham.

Graham's book *The Intelligent Advisor* is seen by Buffett and many others as the best book about investing ever written. In it, Graham discusses the idea of a 50-50 formula in regard to the right percentage of stocks vs. bonds in your portfolio.

He admits that it "may appear to be an oversimplified 50-50 formula." However, he goes on to say, "Under this plan the guiding rule is to maintain as nearly as practicable an equal division between bond and stock holdings. When changes in the market level have raised the common-stock component to, say, 55 percent, the balance would be restored by a sale of one-eleventh of the stock portfolio and the transfer of the proceeds to bonds. Conversely, a fall in the common-stock proportion to 45 percent would call for the use of one-eleventh of the bond fund to buy additional equities."[3]

Indeed, it is a simple investment allocation. Yet, it is time tested and consistent with the renowned philosophies of both Graham and John Bogle of Vanguard. Bogle, one of my favorites, felt a 50-50 approach made a lot of sense for the defensive investor. He felt it would help restrain the investor from being drawn further and further into common stocks as the market rose to dangerous heights.

In other words, the 50-50 Rule is an interesting way to think about investing wisely and always maintaining a moderate balance between risk and reward.

The 50-50 Rule: Keep Half Your Portfolio in Growth and Half in Income

I like to think of Benjamin Graham's 50-50 Rule as a starting point toward the balance of "buckets" in your portfolio.

Now, let's take this 50-50 approach one step further. As your risk tolerance becomes more conservative over time (as you near retirement and have less stomach for large portfolio swings), it may make sense for you to systematically adjust the balance of your buckets—i.e., increase the percentage you have in the "lower volatility" income bucket and reduce the percentage you maintain in the alternative income and growth buckets. In fact, there's an entire category of investment vehicles that attempt to do that for you.

Target date retirement funds do just that. For example, the Vanguard Target Retirement 2030 Fund adjusts its underlying asset mix between stocks and bonds over time.[4] The closer you get to your target retirement date—the year 2030 in this case—the more conservative the mix of investments will become.

Over time, the percentage of stocks will go down and the percentage of bonds will go up. Today, a fund targeting your retirement in the year 2030 may have approximately 20 to 25 percent in bonds and the other 75 percent in stocks, both U.S. and international.

Let's compare that to a 2015 fund. The Vanguard Target Retirement 2015 Fund does the exact same thing as the 2030, except that this one will have approximately 45 to 48 percent in bonds.

If this approach doesn't appeal to you, you can always stick to the basics of Benjamin Graham's philosophy. This means you essentially always keep a balance of half and half—approximately half invested in the growth bucket and half in the income bucket—keeping your life extra simple. If you have half of your portfolio invested in the stock side of the market when the economy's doing well and the stock market's on a tear, at least half of your assets will participate. Not bad.

Conversely, when the world looks scary, the economy is lagging, and the stock market is going down, half of your portfolio might feel the brunt of a stock market correction. The other half, however, the bond (income bucket) side of the equation, might very well be moving sideways, or possibly going up, thus reducing the overall volatility, bite, and downside pressure of your portfolio. In a manner of speaking, half of your portfolio is exposed to risk while the other half is safe in the storm cellar.

If you look at any U.S. stock market history chart, you will see tremendous growth—especially if the chart goes back to the 1920s. In fact, nearly any chart you look at that goes back nine or more decades will show growth in nearly every possible asset class you can think of. Large stocks, small stocks, international stocks, bonds, gold, housing prices—you name it—all have grown in price over time. And the further you look back in time, the greater the rise will seem when looking at where prices stand today.

To give you an idea of what $1 would have turned into had you invested it in 1926 (until the end of 2012), here's how several different investment categories ended up (percentages below are in terms of average annual returns):

- U.S. small stock total return index—$1 turned into $18,365 (11.9 percent)
- U.S. large stock total return index—$1 turned into $3,533 (9.8 percent)
- U.S. long-term government bonds—$1 turned into $123 (5.7 percent)
- U.S. five-year fixed-term investment—$1 turned into $57 (4.8 percent)
- U.S. 30-day Treasury bills—$1 turned into $21 (3.5 percent)
- Inflation—$1 turned into $13 (3 percent)

So let's say an alien from a faraway planet crash-landed on the corner of Broad Street and Wall Street on a Monday morning a few minutes before the NYSE's opening bell. If he looked at these results and was asked what category he wanted to invest in, he would clearly say, "I want the first one on the list—U.S. small stocks. I want the one that makes the most."

It's very simple, right? Even this alien would understand it. And then if that option were not available to him, he'd choose the next best one. U.S. large stocks, right? From the list above, the U.S. large stock index has returned almost 10 percent per year.

Why should this be any different for you? (See Illustration 9.3.) Alien or not, the math is the same.

Illustration 9.3   Best and Worst Possible Investor Returns

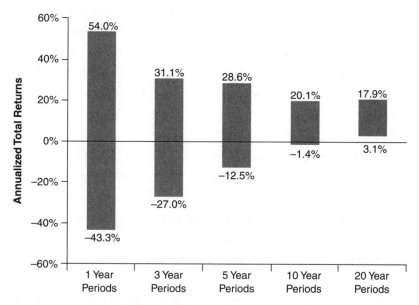

This chart shows the range of S&P returns over 1-, 3-, 5-, 10-, and 20-year holding periods.

Chart created by Strategas Research Partners. Used with permission.

Worst Five-Year Period

If you look at the absolute worst five-year period, from 1926 until 2011, your stock holdings in the S&P 500 could have dropped as much as 12.5 percent annually—provided that you purchased the S&P 500 at the beginning of its worst-ever five-year run. So, even over the course of roughly 85 years, a short five-year period of your money going in the wrong direction can take an extraordinarily difficult emotional and financial toll. This is especially true if you're close to or in retirement.

The very thought of this makes investing your money *purely* in stocks seem very risky. The road to financial gain is fraught with dips, speed bumps, and land mines. During that terrible five-year period when numbers are down more than 12 percent per annum (or over 30 percent in aggregate), it's very difficult to convince yourself to keep your investments all in the growth bucket (stocks, small stocks, etc.).

If you do, you're going to have periods of time that feel like an eternity. Watching your investments fall 30-plus percent in five years—that's pretty tough to stomach. You start to wonder if the days ahead are going to be just as gloomy. "Maybe this time," you think, "America might not get out of its rut. Maybe this time the wars in the Middle East won't end. Maybe we're going to spiral into another dust bowl Great Depression."

There's always the worry of the unknown, and just because America has been a resilient nation in the past doesn't mean the grim reaper won't find us the next time. So it's only natural for most investors to get nervous and anxious when the line dips south, and that's why they don't always have the stomach, fortitude, patience, foresight, and conviction to stay fully invested in stocks.

This is why it's so important to keep in mind Illustration 9.4.

This chart is one of the most interesting pieces of research in the investment industry. Researched by Capital Investment

Illustration 9.4   The Behavioral Effect on Investor Returns

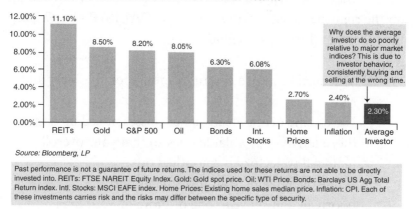

Source: Bloomberg, LP

Past performance is not a guarantee of future returns. The indices used for these returns are not able to be directly invested into. REITs: FTSE NAREIT Equity Index. Gold: Gold spot price. Oil: WTI Price. Bonds: Barclays US Agg Total Return index. Intl. Stocks: MSCI EAFE index. Home Prices: Existing home sales median price. Inflation: CPI. Each of these investments carries risk and the risks may differ between the specific type of security.

This chart, published by Capital Investment Advisors (using market data and research from DALBAR), depicts 20-year annualized returns between 1993 and 2012.

Advisors (and the DALBAR research company), it shows that REITs (real estate investment trusts) were at 11.1 percent, the S&P 500 at 8.2 percent, oil at 8.05 percent, international stocks (EAFE) at 6.08 percent, bonds at 6.3 percent, and housing at 2.7 percent over the 20-year period from 1993 to 2012.

But here's the kicker: the chart shows that, at 2.3 percent a year, the lowest returns belong to the Average Asset Allocation investor (shown to the far right).[5] Even inflation, at 2.5 percent, was higher than the Average Asset Allocation fund investor return. Think that's a bad sign? (Hint: the answer is yes.)

That 2.3 percent is a shockingly low number, considering nearly every major investable asset class is shown in this chart— all of which have done significantly better by themselves. (Actual investor returns were determined by analyzing mutual fund data.) One predominant theory as to why there is such a vast disparity between what "most investments" earn and what individuals earn has to do with individual investors buying, selling, and chasing the wrong asset class, consistently at the wrong time. These practices relate to emotionally "timing the market," leading to the poor overall returns most individual investors are infamous for.

So what's the answer? How do you as an investor not end up on the right-hand side of this infamous DALBAR chart? Keep the following three tips in mind:

- You need to have a careful combination of safety and risk.
- Have some of the steady asset classes mixed in with those terrifyingly volatile ones so that your overall financial trajectory is smoothed out.
- While one area of your investment portfolio does poorly in a given year, one or more of your areas should be increasing in value. As the value of one bucket begins to wane, the value of another bucket turns upward.

Counterbalance is what you're looking for as an investor. You want to smooth out your ride as much as possible and balance those buckets.

The Wes Moss Risk Line Continuum

The easiest way to think of where you stand relative to the rest of the world, from an investment perspective, is to very simply look at the Wes Moss Risk Continuum in Illustration 9.5. You'll see that CDs are on the far left side, at a risk level of 1. On the other end, the far right side, with a risk level of 10, sit the most aggressive and riskiest investments you can find.

If you are an investor occupying the area on the left, you are mostly invested in CDs and money market accounts. If you are an investor fully off to the right side of the continuum, you've invested 100 percent in stocks—particularly small stocks, emerging market stocks, and the most volatile areas of the entire global stock market.

Illustration 9.5 Wes Moss Risk Continuum

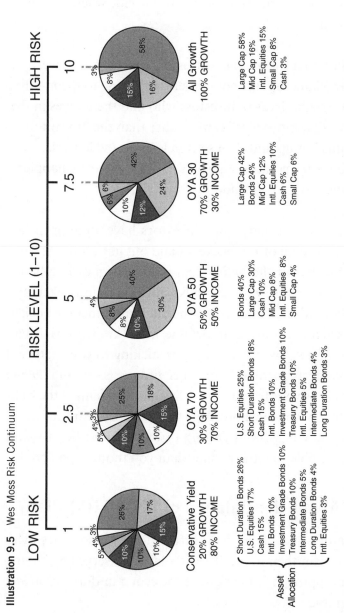

These pie charts show you five examples of different percentage amounts, on a range of preferred risk from 1 (very conservative) to 10 (very aggressive). Pie #1 is a very conservative example (1), Pie #2 is moderately conservative (2.5), Pie #3 is moderate (5), Pie #4 is moderately aggressive (7.5), and Pie #5 is fully aggressive (10).

179

Neither end of the spectrum is a good place to be in its own right. Just like everything else in the world, moderation and balance are king. You want to be somewhere along the continuum.

Here's some information to help you decide where you fit on the continuum:

- I find that the happiest investors (particularly investors age 55 and up) are somewhere very close to the middle.
- More conservative investors who find themselves in the "don't want to lose" camp rather than the "I want big gains" camp find themselves closer to the left side.
- Younger investors, ages 30 to 55, are typically happier closer to the right side.

The key here is that happy investors have an appropriate balance between all of the buckets I laid out in Chapter 8: cash, income, growth, and alternative income. They own various bonds in the income bucket, various stocks in the growth bucket, and various alternative investments in the alternative income bucket.

Find where you are comfortable now (knowing that can change or migrate over time), and try sticking to your personal balance as long as possible. Remember, *balance* is key, and *time-in* as an investor is your friend. If you find and implement the right balance for you, you are more likely to experience years and years of overall growth without getting thrown off the horse—and you might be able to retire sooner than you thought you could.

What About the Balance of My 401(k) Plan?

Accumulators—people in their thirties, forties, and fifties (who have decades for their money to last)—are well served by finding a pie-chart approach to the right of the center in Illustration 9.5, or between the 6 and 9 risk range.

If your main investment assets are in your 401(k) and you have 25 mutual funds to choose from, and every single one of them is set to reinvest dividends—as nearly all 401(k) plans are— then you're adding to this portfolio every time one of your funds pays a dividend or income, in addition to the amount you save each month from your paycheck.

Again, I'm a believer in mastering the middle. So even for those of you in the younger "accumulator" stage, unless you possess great fortitude and are okay with markets going up and down significantly, 10 to 30 percent in any given year, then you don't necessarily want to be at 10 on the risk continuum.

What if you're not an accumulator, and you need to live off of your money now? Then you are officially in the "distribution stage," otherwise known as a distributor. Distributors are primarily in or near retirement—ages 60 and up—and are typically happier between a 2.5 and 7.5 on the risk scale. They tend to put a huge focus on the amount of predictable income that is generated each year from their portfolio. Remember: **it's your portfolio's** *cash flow* **that is the predictable part, not the direction of the stock or bond market.**

Calculating Your Overall Investment Return: Yield + Gain/Loss

By now, you're probably sick of the $10 example, but let's do a super speedy review. You can invest your $10 in two different ways: either it can *grow* a dollar a year for 10 years, leaving you with $20, or it can *pay you a dividend* of a dollar a year, also leaving you with $20. Either way you end up in the same place, but you arrive there through very different vehicles of investment.

The all-growth example is a 10 on the risk line continuum. This method works well if you have a perfect and steady return. But in the real world, the waters aren't usually so calm. You may have a plus 10 percent year, then a minus 15 percent year, then a plus 5 percent year, followed by a minus 3 percent year. So there's little steadiness to an all-growth approach and no reliability in the short term. That makes this method easy to abandon on an emotional level. It's hard to see your hard-earned money fluctuate so much.

On the other hand, if you target a certain yield or income through the DID (dividends, interest, distribution) approach we discussed in Chapter 7, you will know your cash flow or percentage yield at the beginning of every year. In this case, you can target your overall income-only yield (3, 4, or 5 percent), adjust your bucket balance accordingly, and make sure the components inside of each bucket are doing their job of generating steady cash flow.

Remember, on average your income bucket should yield in the 3 to 5 percent range, growth bucket in the 2 to 4 percent range, and the alternative income bucket in the 6 percent range.

Here's an example of targeting on overall portfolio yield:

Balance of the buckets:
- 55% income
- 30% growth
- 15% alternative income

Yield (only) per bucket:
- Income bucket: 4%
- Growth bucket: 3%
- Alternative income bucket: 6%

Here's what the math looks like:

Income 55% × 4% yield

Growth 30% × 3% yield

Alternative income 15% × 6% yield

= **4.00% yield**

Next Example. Now, shift your bucket percentages a bit to the following, assuming the same level of yield for each bucket, and your yield changes.

Balance of the buckets:
- Income bucket: 50%
- Growth bucket: 40%
- Alternative income bucket: 10%

And here's the overall yield:

Income 50% × 4% yield

Growth 40% × 3% yield

Alternative income 10% × 6% yield

= **3.8% overall yield**

Again, what we are solving for here is only the yield part of the equation. One common misconception is that the yield part of the bucket equation is your only return. That's not the case. The yield (cash flow) is the predictable part of the equation. Whether you also will get appreciation out of each bucket (namely the alternative income and growth buckets) largely depends on the economy and stock market in general.

Your overall investment return should be a combination of your yield (the predictable part) *plus* the appreciation (or depreciation, aka gain/loss) in the value of the securities that reside in each bucket. So let's take the overall portfolio yield of 3.8 percent from the preceding example and subject it to an additional equation:

The gain/loss of the underlying investments in each bucket:

- Income bucket: 1%
- Growth bucket: 8%
- Alternative income bucket: 3%

(50% × 1% gain) + (40% × 8% gain) + (10% × 3 % gain)
= 4% overall gain

Now, to calculate the *overall investment return*, here's what the math looks like:

overall investment return = yield + gain/loss

So in this case:

3.8% + 4% = an overall investment return of 7.8%

Now 7.8 percent is a number I can stand behind!

Finding Yourself on the Risk Continuum

Let's say you buy into the bucket approach to income investing. Clearly, you must be a smart and happy person! So, what's next? Consider these three questions:

1. How much time do you have until you need to live off of the money (distribution phase)?
2. What percentage do you allocate to each bucket?
3. What's the risk associated with the balance that you choose?

This goes back to my continuum. It's a great starting point for understanding your personal balance.

If you are 40, how much time do you have as an investor? Well, unless you've been a power-saver since the age of 20, you have roughly 20 to 25 years before you'll likely be in a position of complete financial freedom, having the ability to retire. Then you'll have another 20 to 25 years in retirement. This means you will effectively have a half-century of investing in front of you.

A half-century is a long time horizon. Just remember this before you decide on the balance of your buckets. More years as investor means you will have more time to participate when our economy and stock market has good years. **So unless you are completely afraid of taking any risk whatsoever, make sure you don't ignore the growth bucket,** even if it's the most volatile bucket of the four.

"Anything less than a 10-year horizon is just speculation."

—John Bogle

The quote above is one my favorite investment quotes of all time. I realize that the quote might sound a little idealistic, but not when taken within the context of the turbulent stock market and the economy we experienced (aka: suffered) from 2000 to 2010.

Yet, it is difficult for us as humans to think ahead 50 years. Like all animals, we have that day-to-day survival instinct deep inside of us. That instinct was crucial when we were still running from lions. Unfortunately, it doesn't serve us quite as well amongst the wolves of Wall Street.

Investing is truly something that should be done over your entire lifetime. Ten years can admittedly sound like a heck of a long time today, but not once you take a step back and think about the fact that you're 30, 40, or 50, and might live until you're 90 or 100!

Age-Old Advice: A By-the-Decade How To

If you want some age-old advice on how to balance your buckets, follow my by-the-decade suggestions below:

At Age 40

Put 30 percent in your income bucket, 60 percent in the growth bucket, and 10 percent in the alternative income bucket.

How much of this pays "income"? Great question. One hundred percent of the income bucket pays income—that means 30 percent of your portfolio. One hundred percent of the alternative income bucket pays some sort of income, so that's another 10 percent. That puts us at 40 percent, which means you own your age in income. Mission accomplished!

From there, 50 percent of the growth bucket should be dividend-paying stocks that pay income. That 50 percent in "dividend income" that comes from the growth bucket equals another 30 percent of your total portfolio paying you an income stream, which means another full 30 percent of your overall portfolio is paying you some level of income. All of a sudden, despite only being 40 years old, 70 percent of your assets are giving you income to some degree. While you'll actually be reinvesting, and reinvesting, and reinvesting that income for many years to come, it's still very exciting to see that you'll be able to get used to a consistency of cash flow.

At Age 50

Put 40 percent in the income bucket, 50 percent in the growth bucket, and 10 percent in the alternative income bucket.

Again, which parts are paying you income? One hundred percent of the income bucket, 100 percent of the alternative income bucket, and two-thirds of the growth bucket. Added all up, that means 83 percent of your portfolio is paying you an income.

At Age 60

Put 45 percent in the income bucket, 45 percent in the growth bucket, and 10 percent in the alternative income bucket.

At this point, we don't even have to do any math because I want 100 percent of your portfolio to be paying dividend-paying income.

For the rest of your life, age 60 and above, you should be a 100 percent income investor. I love that rule! Everything should pay you an income. Let's make that your mantra here. **Everything should be paying you an income from age 60 on.** Obviously, there are no absolutes, but if you stick to this mindset, you'll be glad you did.

If You Don't Like Your Risk, Modify It

Many of the examples listed above fall into the "moderate risk" category, anywhere from a 4 to a 7.5 on the risk continuum. How do you change that? Well, there are two ways to increase or modify the risk and expected return of your portfolio.

1. Shift a higher percentage from the income bucket over to the riskier buckets. The growth bucket or alternative income bucket. The less you put in the income bucket, the less predictable, steady, and contained your overall returns will be. The upside goes up, but so does the downside.
2. Change the risk/reward scenario. The risk and volatility perspective of your overall portfolio also adjusts due to the components you use inside your buckets.

If you decide on a percentage to put in a bucket—for example, 50 percent into the growth bucket—what does that composition look like? Should you own stocks like Apple, or is it better to own utility stocks like Southern Company? Looks like we'd better explore. Down into the bucket we go!

Into the Bucket: Taking a Look at Stock Categories

Inside the growth bucket, you have all kinds of different stock categories to choose from. The main categories are U.S., international, and emerging markets stocks. Within the U.S. category, you can use large stocks, small stocks, and midsize stocks. On the more conservative side of the ledger, you would gravitate toward larger companies that are less cyclical (referred to as *noncyclicals*).

I mentioned these previously when speaking about industries in the SHUT index—staples (consumer staple type companies like Procter & Gamble, Colgate, Clorox, Coca-Cola), healthcare companies (Eli Lilly and Bristol-Myers Squibb), utility companies (Consolidated Edison and Southern Company), and telecommunications (AT&T and Verizon).

These companies are within sectors that are not as highly impacted when the economy fluctuates when compared to more cycle sectors (I'll explain these in a minute). For instance, in a bad economy you still run your heater when it's cold, drink Diet Coke, and use Clorox bleach with your laundry.

These areas of the economy just don't fluctuate much—they aren't very cyclical. Hence, these are industries we consider to be noncyclicals. Sounds amazing, right? Why don't we all just buy those? Well, they often don't have as much *growth* potential.

I like to use Southern Company as an example. It's a conglomerate of power companies in multiple states: Georgia, Mississippi, Alabama, and Florida. For our purposes, let's use Georgia.

Southern Company already supplies the power for most customers in the entire state of Georgia. Are they able to double their sales in the way a company like Apple could by coming out with a new product? The answer is no. They are reliant upon people moving to Georgia to use the service they are already providing. Quite frankly, it's very difficult for them to increase or decrease their revenue significantly in any given period. They are a staple in your budget, and their investment value reflects that fact.

To compensate for slower rates of growth, noncyclical companies tend to pay out more of the profits they generate in the form of stock dividends. Hence, you see that one of the highest-paying sectors in stock market is utility companies. They pay anywhere from 3.5 to 5 percent in dividend yield. Not too shabby.

Conversely, think of the more cyclical areas of the economy and stock market. Again, remember my acronym—MEDFIT (materials, energy, discretionary, financials, industrials, and technology).

As an example, I like to look at home builders, who are part of a highly cyclical industry. In 2005 or 2006, did you know any contractors who were out of work? Probably not. New housing starts were running at a pace of over 2 million new homes built annually in America (by 2006). During the Great Recession and housing collapse, that number went down to about 400,000 homes. So we had a 75 to 80 percent drop. Think all those contractors were still working? Nope.

Now imagine the impact that had on housing stocks! Yikes. Like home building, pure growth companies like Google, Amazon, and Facebook can have delicious upsides, but if they go out of favor, imagine what can happen to their stock.

For some context: in 2007 when nearly everyone's smartphone was a BlackBerry, BlackBerry stock soared above $200 a share (from about $20 a share in 2003). As I write this book, BlackBerry trades around $6 a share. So $20 to $200, then down to $6. That's cyclical. (Not to mention bad news for BlackBerry.)

Bonds in the Bucket

In the income bucket, what kind of bonds should you own? There are many kinds of bonds, and not all are created equal. Let's differentiate between some of the types so you can decide which ones make sense for you.

Some bonds available yield less than 1 percent (short-term Treasuries) and others yield nearly 20 percent (bonds issued by some car and insurance companies, for example). So which do you select? The answer is somewhere in between. Here are some bond-oriented income strategies you can combine to find a happy medium.

Investment-Grade Corporate Bonds

Investment-grade corporate bonds are debt instruments issued by corporations to raise money for various reasons. They are IOUs to you as an investor from the company issuing them, with a promise of a coupon payment each month, quarter, or year, and a promise to pay the original issue amount back at maturity. Investment-grade means that the rating agencies have given that bond a minimum rating of BBB or above (ratings from agency to agency may vary).

Over the past 10 years or so, these bonds have yielded (on average) about 1.5 percent more than government-issued debt (Treasuries), but at times can have significantly higher yield than Treasuries, sometimes 2 to 4 percent above. This will depend heavily on the interest rate and economic environment. You can hold these bonds directly as individual bonds, through bond ETFs or index funds, or use an actively managed bond mutual fund.

High-Yield Corporate Bonds

High-yield corporate bonds (familiarly called junk bonds) are corporate-issued debt with a credit rating below BBB. Although the phrase "junk bond" doesn't leave most investors feeling cozy at night, strategic use of high-yield bonds can enhance your income—and if owned in a diversified manner—through the use of an ETF (exchange-traded fund) or mutual fund—the risk can be greatly mitigated.

Due to their lower credit rating, high-yield bond issuers pay a premium yield compared to government and investment grade debt. High-yield bonds may pay you a great deal of interest but carry heavy default risk, and even though you may receive a very high level of interest (5 percent to 8 percent and even higher), the price of your bond may drop or even go to zero if the issuer/company goes belly up. Consider hedging your default risk by owning an ETF or mutual fund with hundreds of underlying positions rather than just owning a handful of individual high-yield bonds.

Municipal Bonds

Municipal bonds are debt instruments issued by local governments to fund the cost and operation of basic public services and projects such as water/sewer projects, toll facilities, roads, bridges, hospitals, and other municipally funded operations. Typically, the interest payments you get from these bonds are funded by the people who use the services: drivers paying tolls, families paying their water/sewer bill, and various state and local taxes.

Municipal bonds are unique because they typically offer yields exempt from federal and state taxes (provided you live in the state of issuance). Given the tax-free interest on these bonds, investors in high tax brackets (the 33 or 39.6 percent brackets) are often able to "keep" more of their income when compared to similar corporate bonds whose interest is whittled down due to taxes.

Municipals are rated by agencies just like corporate bonds and carry varying default risks depending on the issuer. However, think about what it would take for people to stop paying their taxes, tolls, or their utility bills. As my grandmother always said, "People always pay the sewer bill when the toilet bowl starts backing up!"

TIPS

You might also consider Treasury inflation-protected securities (TIPS). We talked briefly about these in the last chapter: they are issued by the U.S. government and attempt to provide three things: safety, yield, and protection against rising future costs (inflation). TIPS are auctioned by the government several times a year, depending on maturities, and are kept at fixed interest rates.

Your TIPS will pay you a consistent yield over time (depending on the maturity) and adjust for inflation. If CPI (the consumer price index) starts going through the roof, never fear: your TIPS will adjust upward. In the event of deflation (where CPI actually goes down), your TIPS will have a negative adjustment. They are traded in the open market, which leaves their price subject to fluctuation. Without having to go directly to the Treasury to purchase TIPS, look at the Barclay's index ETF (TIP) or Vanguard's TIP mutual fund (VIPSX).

I Bonds

I Bonds work similarly to TIPS and are issued directly by the Treasury, but as an individual you can only buy $10,000 worth of I Bonds in a given year. Instead of a specific maturity, they work on an accrual basis, accumulating interest until you choose to cash them in.

Yields now on I Bonds can be pretty low, sometimes lower than 1 percent, but there will be more to the story as I Bonds adjust for inflation, moving up in line with the consumer price index (CPI). So if CPI was at 4 percent, an I Bond owner with a

1 percent interest rate would receive 1 percent *plus* the 4 percent adjustment for a grand total of 5 percent. Not bad for a government bond.

Floating Rate Bonds

These are a form of corporate or high-yield bonds that have flexible interest rates. This makes them very different from most of the other bond categories. Because the interest paid to you can "float," it means that as interest rates migrate up over the next five years (or more)—as I expect them to do—you are not locked into an exceedingly low interest rate. If interest rates in general migrate higher over the next several years, floating rate bonds have a good chance of *avoiding* the negative impact of the bond-price to interest-rate seesaw effect.

My Advice on How Best to Diversify

You should own a diverse basket of "bonds" depending on your needs and risk tolerance. Conservative investors who place safety over yield should put their emphasis on corporate bonds, high-quality municipal bonds, and government-issued TIPS, while more aggressive income investors could choose to focus on corporate, high-yield, and floating rate bonds as they seek higher yields.

It's important to note that diversification is key with all types of bonds. That's why I recommend broadly diversified exchange-traded funds (ETFs) and actively managed corporate and municipal funds with ultra-low internal fees.

Whether you prefer stocks or bonds, cyclicals or noncyclicals, TIPS or high-yield bonds, MLPs stocks or floating rate bonds, REITs or Energy Royalty Trusts, or any of the other countless investment vehicles, always keep in mind the balance between risk, safety, and reward.

Some risks are worth it, but only be as risky as you have to be. Investing is simple, not easy. Success in any field, including investing, takes time—you can't sprint a marathon. Find the pace that's right for you, and let it carry you toward an early retirement.

CHAPTER 10

Avoid the Major Pitfalls of Investing

'll never forget the morning Ryan Pepper walked into my office with a spreadsheet and a smile. At 64 years old, he's one of my happiest retirees: fit, healthy, and in love with life. That morning Ryan walked briskly to my desk and handed me a piece of paper.

"What's this, Ryan?" I asked.

"It's a spreadsheet I made," he said, grinning from ear to ear. "In 1997. Every year since I've gone in and entered my total savings from the year."

I looked it over, and the first year's entry immediately jumped out at me: $32,000. That's how much Ryan had in savings in 1997.

My jaw dropped. Not because I'd never seen 32 Gs (at Capital Investment Advisors we manage well over $1 billion in client assets, after all). My jaw dropped because I knew how much the Peppers' savings are worth today: *$1.35 million.*

How did he and his wife, Allie, get there in just 16 years? They did it by avoiding the things that can go wrong—the pitfalls of bad investing. Doing this requires deft psychological navigation of the market, as well as having a solid philosophy for your investment strategies.

This chapter is about avoiding the major pitfalls of investing. I'll show you how to emulate the Peppers so that, when you come see me in 16 years to retire, your 2014 spreadsheet will make my jaw drop just as much as theirs did.

Made Mistakes in the Past?
It's Not Too Late to Start Over

Avoiding pitfalls is an essential part of successful investing. Doing so takes an understanding of the psychological factors that so often play into investment mistakes. Perhaps it won't surprise you to learn those mistakes typically occur when people act in the *opposite* way of the five money secrets.

Nowhere is this truer than secret #2: Figure out how much money you need to have saved before you retire. The biggest pitfall of retirement planning is hands down the failure to save enough money. I see it time and again with people who call in to *Money Matters* or walk into the CIA offices. Accumulating those savings takes more time than any of the other secrets. If you were planning to neglect any of the five, this is not the one you'd want to pick.

That's the big one. The good news is: if you missed out on one of the other five, it's more easily repaired. For instance, you can always pick up another core pursuit or two (secret #1)—start taking cooking or art classes, try mountain biking, or study portrait photography. Why not?

Suffering under a big mortgage is another common pitfall, but you can fix that by paying off your mortgage—even if it means going into economic shutdown mode (more on that momentarily). Furthermore, you can refinance from a 30-year mortgage down to a 15-year, make extra payments, and—even if you don't start until age 50—you can still be free and clear by 65.

Having multiple income sources can be achieved by working longer or having a part-time job. And you can always learn to be an income investor, as I showed you in Chapters 8 and 9.

So you can overcome the pitfalls of not learning secrets 1, 3, 4, and 5 early on in life. But not having saved enough money (secret #2) is a deep one that's hard to climb out of. This is why the Peppers are such important role models for you.

Live Like Ryan Pepper:
Happy, Active, and Free

Ryan Pepper lives life! He just finished running the Louisiana Ironman. If you've never heard of an Ironman, it's the most grueling kind of triathlon you can possibly do.

How grueling? A 2.4-mile swim followed by a 112-mile bicycle ride, topped off with a 26.2-mile run. You know a race is tough when they put the swimming portion first so people don't drown! But that doesn't bother Ryan Pepper. At 62, he set a PR (personal record) by shaving an hour off his time. An hour! He went from 15½ hours down to 14½. Think about how long that is. You could almost get two full nights of sleep in the same span. Ryan was competing for approximately eight REM cycles.

Talk about a man who lives by the wise words often attributed to Abraham Lincoln: "In the end, it's not the years in your life that count. It's the life in your years." There's no doubt Ryan Pepper is living with a tremendous amount of purpose.

What about Allie, Ryan's lovely wife? She loves their active and dynamic lifestyle of traveling, visiting their grown children, and supporting Ryan in his events. This is a very active and happy couple, fully engaged in putting as much life into their years as possible.

The Peppers' mortgage will be paid off in the next year or two. When they "retire" from full-time work in about a year, they will have several different streams of income. Ryan is also going to continue to work part-time as a consultant to bring in an extra $20,000 to $40,000 per year. Why? Because he knows how powerful an extra income source can be on the quest to an early retirement.

The Peppers have been income investors for many years now. They believe in yield; they believe in steadiness of income. They know that when they retire, they can count on a certain steady level of cash flow coming from their investments. They'll have a small pension. They'll both have a modest amount of social security. And by the way, we've been planning this for years now, and they understand from a cash flow (yield) perspective that they can easily fill the gap—FTG—when it comes to spending.

But enough about that. How did they go from $32,000 to $1.35 million in 16 years? It took some doing. Let me explain.

It Wasn't Always This Good: How Ryan and Allie Turned Their Life Around

Between 1984 and 1994, Ryan worked for a company called Digital. During those years, Ryan and Allie used to spend a lot of money on what they would now consider "junk"—frivolous habits combined with credit card and student loan debt. According to Ryan and Allie, they loved to spend and basically spent whatever they earned. They just kind of forgot to save.

The Peppers were headed toward the unhappy group of retirees. In fact, they weren't just headed toward unhappiness—they were on a collision course.

During the 1980s and early 1990s, Ryan made a decent living: somewhere in the neighborhood of $50,000 to $60,000 a year. Yet, all they could manage to do was break even. Then, between 1994 and 1997, he got a job consulting for a company called

Convergent Media Systems and started making around $110,000 a year. Allie was a preschool teacher bringing in $18,000 a year, working about 30 hours a week for a small private school.

One day Allie walked by the kitchen table and happened to notice Ryan's 401(k) statement. It said they only had $32,000. "Ryan!" she exclaimed. "We haven't been saving any money. What the heck are we doing?"

That was the moment they changed their lifestyle. That was the day they started walking on the path that leads to a happy retirement. How old were they on that portentous day?

Allie was 47 and Ryan was 48.

So they weren't fresh out of the crib, if you catch my drift. And they *still* managed to turn their retirement—and their lives—around.

Ryan's income continued to slowly grow at his job. In the early 2000s, Allie went to work for Gillman Insurance Company; by 2004, her income had gone up to roughly $25,000 a year. She quit in 2011 after having peaked at $42,000.

In the year 2000, Ryan left the software-consulting world to become a financial advisor at American Express Advisors. It didn't go so well. He basically made no income for the year, hated it, and went back to consulting in 2001, and that's when his income started to step up a little bit—he was making about $140,000 to $150,000 a year working for Accenture. As of 2013, he was making around $220,000 annually.

The Peppers went from having $32,000 in 1997 to $810,000 by 2007—just 10 years. To be fair, $200,000 was from an inheritance, but that still required them to save more than $600,000 with no outside help. Where did that money come from, you ask? From their own savings, growth, blood, sweat, and tears.

The Peppers started by avoiding all the psychological pitfalls of investors. Wouldn't you like to be a Pepper, too?

Fear and Greed: Two Powerful Emotions
That Can Ruin You Financially

On October 6, 2008, I remember seeing brilliant financial strate-gist Jim Cramer on the *Today Show* telling people point-blank to take any money they might need in the next five years out of the stock market, because he was worried about another precipitous stock market decline.[1] Interestingly, he was partially right: from October 6, 2008, until March 9, 2009 (slightly more than five months), the market did continue to drop to the tune of negative 34 percent for the Dow Jones Industrial Average.

But what happened over the course of a full five-year period? From October 2008 until October 2013? Despite the large drop at the beginning of that time period, the stock market was actually up by 50 percent at the end of it. In Cramer's defense, he did say that if you had *more* than a five-year time horizon and could with-stand another correction, it was best to hold on, but this is still an example of fear and emotion driving your financial decisions.

My point here is twofold.

1.   Even Jim Cramer was afraid people would lose more money, because by that October morning in 2008 he had already seen the market go down nearly 30 percent in a year's time.
2.   Even though he warned of a further correction and was right, if investors had held on over that five-year period, they ultimately would have made 50 percent in the Dow Jones Industrial Average. But scores of investors over the final months of 2008 and early 2009 fled the stock market in droves.

What happened from March 9, 2009, to March 9, 2013, the next four-year period? The Dow rallied from 6,547 all the way to 14,397 on March 8, 2013. That's almost 8,000 points to the upside, or approximately 120 percent!

Investors, in mass, were afraid. So they made emotional decisions to get out of the market—just in time for it to go up by over 100 percent.

On the other side of the pendulum are the periods dictated by greed—the fear of not making enough. We all know what this looks like. These investors say to themselves, "Hey, my neighbor said he made more than 30 percent on his investments over the last six months. I need to take some extra risk in my portfolio to try to keep up!" Unfortunately, that type of mentality can bleed into every other area of their life. "My colleague owns three condos in Florida, so I need to go buy one." "My sister just bought a bigger house; isn't it time we got a bigger house too?" And so on.

When there's a housing or stock market bubble like there was in the late 1990s, and people notice stocks climbing 20 and 30 percent over a matter of weeks or months, they get greedy. Their fundamentals of diversification and balance are supplanted by greed, and they start chasing the hottest areas of the market just in time for them to blow up.

This is a well-documented psychological phenomenon over the course of history. Whether it's tulips in seventeenth-century Holland, condos in Las Vegas, or the tech bubble, when the value of an asset goes up, investors in mass start to think *they* need more of it. As the buying herd gains momentum, the asset's price skyrockets. Then, all of a sudden, everyone realizes it's not worth as much as they thought and there's a rush to the exit door.

So the price for an asset that is in a bubble goes from $10 to $50 to $1,000—and then crashes back down to $50. It's been happening since the first instance of recorded money, and probably long before that.

Other Psychological Pitfalls

You've no doubt heard of the *herd mentality*, which is often fueled by greed, fear, or a combination of the two. "Hey, everyone's getting out. I need to get out, too!" and "Hey, everyone's getting in. I need to get in, too!" are both examples of different types of herding.

Another psychological pitfall is known as *benchmarking*. There are so many markets around the world: the large-cap U.S. market, the small-cap U.S. market, the energy market, the gold market, the European markets, the Asian markets, the Australian market—I could go on. If you were so inclined, you could follow the price of oil, copper, gold, palladium, and even bitcoins (if you're the Winklevoss twins).

There are hundreds of benchmarks to look at besides the S&P 500 and the Dow, and there's always going to be a winner in any given year. There are so many of these to choose from, no one can ever know ahead of time what the best market around the world will be.

Thus, benchmarking is the phenomenon of always seeing something better—the greenbacks are always greener on the other side. "Hey, my portfolio is up 12 percent this year, and that's good, but the European stock market is up 25, shouldn't I be over there?" Benchmarking can run you ragged and lead you to constant disappointment, which leads back to greed-based herding behavior.

The biggest mistake I see is investors *relying on past performance*. That's when an investor takes a list of 20 or 30 choices and looks only at the percentage returns. "Oh, that fund did 22 percent last year, this fund only did 5. I'd better buy the one that did 22." The decision is made without having any idea if that 22 percent is good, bad, or in line with what it should have been. No research is done to see what sectors were responsible for the 22 percent gain. Investors end up chasing an investment based on what it *has done*, not understanding *why* an investment did what it did, or what its prospects are for the *next* five years.

I've seen many investors select a fund because it averaged 7 or 8 percent a year for the past several years without asking if the fundamentals of the investments inside the fund have shifted dramatically for future years. For all they know, it might be next to impossible for that increase to replicate itself.

It's very important to understand the investments you own. That's one of the reasons I'm so emphatic about using my bucket approach—it promotes greater understanding of what you own, while still keeping things simple. As an investor, it's easy to understand that you own stocks in one bucket, bonds in another bucket, and alternative income investments in another bucket. Furthermore, the bucket approach keeps you aware of the various kinds of assets you own within each bucket, giving you a better understanding of how each bucket should perform in various market environments.

In other words, the bucket approach gives you an easy, no-fuss way to comprehend what's under the hood. You can understand what you actually own rather than "blindly" looking at the track record of a fund, ETF, or stock.

Anchoring is another psychological pitfall. Let's say you've had a stock in the family for many years and you have an emotional attachment to it. Or maybe your mom bought you some shares of a stock when you turned 13 and you don't want to sell because you're comfortable with them. That comfort and sentiment doesn't make it a *safe* stock or even a good stock to continue to own. It just means you're comfortable with that stock. Psychologically, you may think it's safe, when in fact it could be a disaster waiting to happen.

I've also seen people fall victim to *narrow framing*. This is when you make decisions without understanding all the implications. Perhaps you worked for Coca-Cola, Home Depot, or Cisco. You like the company and think you understand what they're about—which is fine—but you have a tremendous amount of money invested in that one company. It's 40, 50, or even 80 percent of your investments because you "understand" it—or at least, you think you do.

Again, it's not a safe stock just because you understand the company that it represents. This is a result of a psychological disconnect between fundamentally sound investing and a false sense of comfort. Don't let these psychological tricks hurt you.

Another psychological pitfall can be caused by the influx of media (think 24/7 news outlets like CNBC, CNN, Fox News, MSNBC, Bloomberg, you name it). The news can very quickly skew your own emotional pendulum between fear and greed. Back in July of 2010 when the world was watching the onset of a complete financial crisis in the relatively tiny country of Greece and worrying about the repercussions for all of Europe, I remember seeing author and financial forecaster Robert R. Prechter, Jr. talking about his forecast for the stock market.

The Dow was somewhere around 9,600, and Prechter was warning that there was going to be a major drop in the next several years—a drop to Dow 1000 (about 90 percent). Nearly three and a half years after his prediction (also reported in the *New York Times*), the Dow was trading more than 65 percent higher. So, he called for a 90 percent drop and instead the market went up by more than 65 percent. How's that for sensationalism?

News channels are trying to report the news, but they're also trying to get ratings. Talking heads and pseudo-experts with extreme viewpoints are going to get the most news attention. If Prechter's view had been that the Dow was going to move up and down within reason, where's the scandal?

Having a balanced opinion isn't sexy, but we know that over time the symmetry and balance of the bucket approach helps to eliminate many of these emotional pitfalls, for two reasons.

1. Income and cash flow—now both within your control. If you don't need it, you reinvest it. If you do need it, you start taking it. You're okay with some fluctuation in the value of these buckets because you're still getting your income from your bucket as a whole.
2. The balance makes it easier for you to have at least one of your buckets working well at any given time—and perhaps multiple buckets firing on all cylinders. This will help prevent you from falling prey to herding, anchoring, benchmarking, media sensationalism, and the long list of other insidious psychological pitfalls.

When in Doubt, Stick to the Bucket Approach

Back in 2008, before I knew them, the Peppers were invested very heavily in stocks (near a 10 on the risk continuum). The great work they had done from 1997 to 2008 was being erased as their portfolio was down by more than 35 percent. Instead of panicking and jumping out of the market completely, they employed a balanced bucket approach. They focused on what they could control—their balance and their portfolio income.

This helped them stay with a balanced investment plan that included dividend-paying stocks, various types of bonds, and several energy-related investments that continued to pay distributions. This balance was key to helping them *stay the course.*

Subsequently, the stock market rebound of 2009–2012 changed the situation. The Peppers were finally hitting their stride as power-savers, and their investments began to rebound in price.

Their kids had been out of college now since the earlier part of 2002, which helped Ryan begin to fully max out his 401(k) at work. He even put another 15 percent of his money into buying discounted stock from his employer.

As I mentioned earlier, the Peppers inherited around $200,000 when their parents passed, but other than that, their journey from $32,000 to $1.35 million was due to systematically saving and investing close to 30 percent a year and avoiding the psychological pitfalls of investing that I just described. They stuck to the bucket approach and allowed their own savings to grow to a level where they can now retire *whenever they choose*. Because of good decisions, their reservoir of savings will now generate income for them when they do decide to retire. And trust me: they'll be retiring soon!

Another pitfall you should put on your radar is the potential of being charged fees for your investment decisions. Avoid costs that can ding your bottom line. Most investors pay fees on fees, which can end up taking away 5 to 30 percent of their return per year. It's a slow, extremely leaky bucket phenomenon. Don't let it happen to you.

The slick creativity of financial institutions to invent and implement fees would be impressive if it weren't also such a hindrance to the retirement savings of hardworking people around the country. The first step to avoiding these fees is to identify them, and I've come up with some guidelines to help you do it. I call it the "seven layer dip of fees" (see below).

The Seven Layer Dip of Fees

As an investor, you sometimes need to remember the Serenity Prayer—"God, grant me the serenity to accept the things I cannot change, courage to change the things I can, and wisdom to know the difference." Many facets of investing are beyond our control. Fortunately, we can do something about investment fees. Which is good, because fees can seriously hinder your rate of return. As you build and tweak your portfolio, keep an eye out for what I call the Seven Layer Dip of Fees.

1. **Mutual fund fees.** There are plenty of good mutual funds that don't charge large fees. Your investment advisor should offer you a way to have access to "no-load" (funds that do not have an upfront or backend fee) or institutional share classes. No-load funds have no barriers to entry or exit, and institutional share classes generally have *much* lower annual fees.

2. **Mutual fund surrender penalties.** Surrender penalties are a tricky way for a mutual fund company to force you to leave your money in its fund to avoid paying a hefty fee to get the money out. Penalty fee periods can be as long as eight years or more and cost as much as 8 percent of the value of your investment! Avoid these mutual funds like the plague!

3. **Brokerage trading commissions.** The days of paying a few hundred dollars to execute a securities trade are over. You can open an online brokerage account and make a trade for less than $15. Independent advisors can trade on behalf of their clients for as little as $8 a trade. Charles Schwab, TD Ameritrade, and Fidelity are great places to start.

4. **Internal mutual fund operating costs.** Mutual fund managers make their living from the fund's *expense ratio*. The charges vary greatly from fund to fund. High-priced, "actively" managed funds, that seek to outperform the market (and rarely do), are in the 1 to 1.5 percent range. Index funds that attempt to "passively" track the return of the market require much fewer people and less research to run (and actually outperform the majority of "active funds"). They also have much lower fees, in the .07 to 0.50 percent range.

5. **Wrap management fees.** In an effort to appear more fee conscious, many big firms offer "fee-based" accounts. This is an attempt to mitigate brokerage costs associated with the big firms. But be wary—the management fee (generally a percentage of assets under management) goes to the broker and is layered on top of mutual fund fees and account fees charged by many of the big banks/brokerage firms. At the end of the day, you can still end up with an investment cost of more than 2 percent—on what is supposed to be a fee-conscious investment account.

6. **Markups on bonds and new-issue securities.** Advisors at big bank/brokerage firms have the ability to sell you individual bonds and stocks from their firm's inventory. The dirty little secret: advisors are allowed to "mark up" the price of the bond or other security when they buy it for you and keep the difference. This can be a hard fee to quantify as the commission is often built into the price of the security. To add to the pain, brokers can also "mark up" the price when they sell the security for you—a double whammy of fees!

7. **12b-1 fees.** Known as 12b-1 fees, these are marketing fees that mutual fund companies give back to advisors and firms that put their clients in the fund. There is a lot of debate right now about how 12b-1 fees should be disclosed and whether or not they are appropriate; just be aware that this is a sneaky layer in the dip of fees. It tastes good to them, but not you.

Brokerage firms, big banks, mutual funds, and investment firms can't help you manage your money for free—they have to charge for their expertise, counsel, and time. However, it has been proven that one of the biggest killers of investment performance over time is paying *excessive* fees. So ask your advisors, or brokers, exactly how they are getting paid, and all the ways that you are paying for their service. The fewer layers of *dip* you have to work through, the more money you will have left over in retirement. Now, who brought the chips?

Divorce: The Most Expensive Mistake You'll Ever Make

As callous as it sounds, another pitfall is divorce. Barring unusual circumstances, staying married will definitely save you money. Think of it this way. I recently went out to dinner and was introduced to a friend of a friend. He was about 60 years old, and evidently he's been divorced four times.

You can pretty much say with great conviction that there's no way this poor guy can retire early or happy. The economics of divorce are pretty simple. You divide your assets in half each time you go through it. So if you get divorced four times, even if you started with $20 million, you're going to be down to $1.25 million by the end. And something tells me this guy didn't start with $20 million.

Divorce economics—getting your net worth cut in half—is brutal. There's a reason more millionaires in *The Millionaire Next Door* are still married and have never been divorced. It's also reflected in my happiness study: simply put, **it's easier to be a happy retiree if you are married.** The numbers don't lie.

Don't Get Comfortable: Rebalance Your Buckets Every 6 to 12 Months

I've seen so many retirees and preretirees make the mistake of not rebalancing their accounts, and it breaks my heart. They simply don't pay attention to their investments. Remember: knowledge is power.

Let's say your buckets are set up so you essentially have a 50-50 Rule of stocks and bonds. Five years pass without you ever looking at your portfolio, and all of a sudden it has become 75 percent stocks and 25 percent bonds—but you've never rebalanced your investments. Unwittingly, you have an extraordinarily different risk profile today than you did five years ago, just by the virtue of one area growing rapidly and another area not growing rapidly.

If you never rebalance your 401(k) or your investment accounts, you run the risk of the market itself taking you out of balance. **Adopt a philosophy of checking your portfolio every 6 to 12 months** to make sure you're maintaining an appropriate "balance of the buckets" for you and your family.

A Lack of Liquidity: Don't Let It Happen to You

Another big mistake a lot of investors make is having investments that, by nature of the product that they are sold by an insurance salesperson, stockbroker, or financial planner, don't allow them access to their money in the event that they need it. I've seen people really get burned in investments where there's a lack of liquidity, trapping them in the investment for 5 to 15 years—either because there's no market available when they want to sell, or there are significant penalties to access their funds.

An illiquid investment can be a recipe for disaster. I'll be frank: it's one of the reasons I'm not a big fan of annuities. Keep reading and I'll tell you why.

The Truth About Annuities

I'm constantly asked, "What about a variable annuity? I buy it and it guarantees me a steady stream of income in retirement, right?"

I am certainly an advocate of investments that will pay you consistently once your working days are behind you, but I'm not convinced a variable annuity is the best tool for getting the job done.

An annuity is a product sold by insurance companies designed to invest money from an individual. They then pay out a stream of income to that investor over multiple years. A variable annuity promises a minimum return from an "income perspective," plus the possibility of a larger income stream, based on how well the annuity's investments do over time.

Understand the following before buying a variable annuity:

"Real" Versus "Theoretical"

Most variable annuities consist of two pools of money—one "real" and one "theoretical." The *real* pool is what you place in mutual fund-like investments (called subaccounts) within the variable annuity. You can withdraw this entire pool of money at any time—minus, oftentimes, a surrender charge.

The *theoretical* pool is your initial investment amount that grows at a predetermined rate set by the insurance company; for many annuities that rate is 5 percent per year. (By the way, who's backing these rates? Annuities are not insured by the government. Just an FYI.)

But here's the catch: you don't have full access to the theoretical bucket. The theoretical bucket is there for you to take an income stream from *in the future*.

Surrender Charges

Surrender charges can be significant—often between 2 and 10 percent—and can be imposed as long as 10 years after purchase.

Brutal Fees and Commissions

Annuities often come with brutal fees and commissions—the annual expenses average 3 to 3.5 percent. Sales commissions from the original sale of the annuity can range from 4 to 8 percent: a significant incentive for those selling annuities.

Be wary of annuities that promise things like "guaranteed 5 percent income." Annuities with long surrender periods and/or high annual fees lock up your money and then slowly pay it back to you. And what happens if the market does poorly over the next 10 to 20 years and the baby boomer generation needs to collect on the "theoretical bucket" guarantee all at once?

Stampede! Remember AIG? Yikes!

The benefits of a variable annuity generally don't justify the high annual fees and surrender penalties. Of course, there are always exceptions. For example, if you're panic-prone, they might help you avoid making bad investment timing decisions. As always, though, be careful of a "free lunch"—there's no such thing. And if you are ever thinking about buying an annuity, have a third party (someone not working on commission) give you an objective view of the benefits and costs of doing so.

How to Find Objective Advice

Where do you find someone who provides financial planning without getting paid sales commissions? That's easy. NAPFA: The National Association of Personal Financial Advisors.[2]

This is a network of fee-only financial firms and advisors who specifically do not work on commission or the sale of any particular financial product. In full disclosure, I have been a member for many years—but the website will help you find a fee-only planner near you in any area of the country. All you have to do is enter your zip code in the "locate an advisor" tab.

Here is a description taken directly from the NAPFA website:

The National Association of Personal Financial Advisors (NAPFA) is the country's leading professional association of Fee-Only financial advisors—highly trained professionals who are committed to working in the best interests of those they serve. Since 1983, Americans across the country have looked to NAPFA for access to financial professionals who meet the highest membership standards for professional competency, client-focused financial planning, and Fee-Only compensation.

In other words: they only make a fee if they make money for *you*.

The Wes Moss Economic Shutdown

There are many facets and methods that can help you increase your savings at an accelerated rate, but a key factor is discipline.

One philosophy is to do what the Peppers did. Max out your 401(k) savings every single year and make sure both spouses are working. Another philosophy, and one that Dave Ramsey fans might like, is a bit more extreme. It's called the Wes Moss Economic Shutdown.

There's nothing magical about the economic shutdown, it's simply a dramatic change in your spending and lifestyle habits in order to rapidly get out of debt and save a big chunk of money. It's power-saving on steroids, but don't tell Barry Bonds or Lance Armstrong.

During an "economic shutdown," you don't spend one dime more than required to meet your needs. Here's the plan.

- **Budget.** Figure out how much income you have after taxes. Then, write down *everything* you spend on a monthly and yearly basis. In order to get control of your money, you have to know how much is coming in, how much is going out, and where it's going. A "sorta budget" in your head won't get the job done.

- **Set goals.** How much debt do you want to pay off this year? How much do you want to add to your emergency fund? How much do you need for that down payment on a house? If that goal requires more money than you can wring out of your budget by trimming existing spending, it might be time for an "economic shutdown."
- **Housing.** Move in with your parents and pay zero or minimal rent. If that's not possible, get a roommate—or two.
- **Food.** Pack lunch and eat breakfast before you leave for work. Cook dinner at home—affordable meals that make good leftovers. Kroger and Target are tough to beat for the best deal on groceries.
- **Clothing.** Buy only what you truly need to look presentable in work and social situations. Bonus points if it works for both.
- **Entertainment.** No dinners out, no trips to the movies, no vacations, no expensive nights on the town. Cancel cable TV and Netflix. This is a great time to catch up on your reading, watch that classic movie on DVD borrowed from the library, or invite friends over to play a board game.

I can hear you now, "Weeees, how *long* do I have to *do* this?" Answer: Until you've reached your goal. But that might be sooner than you think.

Do You Believe in Miracles?
Ryan and Allie Pepper Do

I think the Pepper story is a minor miracle. To go from $32,000 to $1.35 million in 16 years is a tremendous feat that very few people in America pull off. For proof of this, one need look no further than today's scary retirement statistics. Did you know:

- **More than one-third of the country isn't saving.** Thirty-five percent of Americans don't contribute to retirement accounts.[3]
- **The ones who have saved haven't saved enough.** Fifty-seven percent of workers report that they and/or their spouse have less than $25,000 in total savings and investments (excluding their homes and defined benefit plans). And 28 percent have less than $1,000 (up from 20 percent in 2009).[4]
- **Many seniors are poor.** One out of every six elderly Americans is already living below the federal poverty line.[5]
- **Men and women are working longer.** A record 33 percent of Americans now plan on working past the age of 70—which makes sense, when you consider they don't have money saved to retire.[6]
- **The cost of healthcare is formidable.** Fifty-one percent of Americans doubt they can pay for medical expenses in retirement.[7]

Those are some depressing statistics—but the Peppers' story sets them in sharp relief. In a world where alarmingly high numbers of Americans aren't saving and don't expect to have enough saved, the Peppers were able to do so in a fairly short period of time. To me, that's more than remarkable; it's inspiring.

You, too, can avoid the pitfalls that have ensnared so many well-intentioned Americans, but don't waste any more time. Every day is another dollar wasted. Get started immediately and fly in the face of the odds. Not only will you be able to retire early—you'll be able to retire happier than you ever dreamed.

PART FOUR

Enjoying the Rest of Your Life

CHAPTER 11

Hobbies, Recreation, Vacations, and So Much More

M eri Murphy was recently featured in the *New York Times.*[1] At 67 years old, she's chosen to spend her retirement traveling the world. She adheres to a strict $65-a-day budget and minimizes insurance costs by using local doctors in the countries she visits. Her social security is $1,567 a month after taxes, and she receives $1,110 a month for a government pension. With $2,677 a month, she is living out her dream to spend time in every country before she dies.

It's not everybody's dream retirement—in fact, it's pretty "out there" for most of us. But what Meri's story proves is that you don't have to be rich to have the retirement of your dreams. You don't have to be a millionaire. But you *do* have to plan for the utility of your money.

For years I've been working with a woman named Nicole Walker who would give Meri a run for her money. Having paid off her house, she has zero debt, a net worth of $900,000, and she's in the middle of a year-and-a-half journey backpacking around the world. She basically took $100,000 of her investment income for the next year and a half, and that's her backpacking fund. Knowing Nicole, she'll probably do the whole thing for closer to $30,000.

Nicole, at 62, retired early and happy by doing all the right things to save the right amount of money to live the life she wants to live. In the meantime, the $900,000 she has saved remains invested and continues generating income for her.

Here's how the numbers work for Nicole:

- $1,750 per month from social security
- $1,000 per month from her pension
- $3,000 per month from investment income (She takes her $900,000 in savings and only withdraws 4 percent per year, equaling $36,000 per year, or $3,000 per month.)
- Total monthly income = $5,750 = backpacking and happiness for Nicole

Nicole is doing exactly what she wants to do with her retirement because she laid the groundwork we've talked about in this book. When the time came, she had the freedom to retire early and happy.

Happiness is freedom. It is the freedom to be healthy and social. It is the freedom to have core pursuits. It's the freedom to enjoy your life. In the grand scheme of things, we're not really on this planet all that long. Why not enjoy the time we have?

The tools in this book are geared toward giving you the economic and financial freedom to unlock all the other possibilities. The happiest retirees have the economic freedom to spend a lot of time doing what is important to them. They're in the *passion zone.* This economic and financial freedom allows them to be fully engaged in their core pursuits around the world.

Take a Trip and See the World

Throughout the course of history, travel has often been considered the purest form of freedom. Even today, you can't do it unless you have the financial means to create that opportunity, and there are still plenty of countries in the world that don't make it easy. Think of North Korea, or the years of travel restrictions between the United States and Cuba. Think about all the other countries with ambiguous restrictions or possible travel warnings from the U.S. State Department. I'm thinking of China, Angola, Algeria, Turkmenistan, Bhutan, Saudi Arabia, Myanmar, and the Maldives.

The point is, throughout history, and even to some degree today, being able to travel freely without limit or hindrance has never been a given. With that in mind, shouldn't we take advantage of it every chance we get? Doesn't it make sense to say that is freedom and that is happiness?

I can't tell you how many of the couples I work with have a blast RVing around the country. They take an RV or pull a camper in a truck and head out on the open road. Even John Steinbeck did it in his book *Travels with Charley: In Search of America.* He understood the feeling, the need to get out and be free.

Connie Wheeler came into my office recently, on the very day she retired from a global electronics firm after 32 years. Her husband, Don, had already retired from the HVAC industry. Guess what they'd like to do? They ride Harleys. Yes. Harleys. Don drives, and Connie rides on the back. They'll go from Atlanta up to New York City, or down to Miami or Daytona.

Sam and Loretta Freeman have traveled to all 48 continental states in their RV. Next year they're finally going to Alaska. They've already decided they'll hit up Madrid after that. Is there a bridge to Europe?

Vicki Hightower went to Moscow for the cultural experience. She took her 16-year-old granddaughter with her, and two of her granddaughter's girlfriends. She showed her granddaughter the Kremlin, bad food, Pepsi, and vodka. At least that's what I remember from my time in St. Petersburg.

The Joy of the Villages

The Quintessential Happy Retiree Lifestyle—All in One Place

Larry and Gail Curcuru are only 58 and 59, respectively, and they have wanted to move to The Villages in Florida for years. When they first became clients 10-plus years ago, they talked about it . . . and talked about it . . . and finally two years ago, they did it.

They are young for The Villages, but they love every minute of it, and they are living out their happiest retirement dreams. Gail recently e-mailed me about how much they love their new life.

She said, "I often tell friends and family, and the occasional stranger, that living here is like living on vacation." She sent me a link to a page of fun facts about The Villages[2] and went on to say, "As you can see from the link, there are lots and lots of golf courses, pools, tennis courts, recreation centers, clubs, activities, and healthcare choices, etc.: all things that were important to us when we selected a place to retire. Of course, our idea of retirement was not to sit in front of a TV or lounge on the front porch swing. Our idea was to be active, have FUN, and feel happy and safe."

Gail is so happy that she was afraid her e-mail sounded "made up." Not so, she said: "This is truly what our life is like here!"

Larry and Gail have tapped into the happiness I want for all of you. You can feel it pouring out of her with each and every word. "It's hard to define happy and what makes you safe," said Gail. "I love when I walk around one of our three town squares and I see couples holding hands, talking with friends, and dancing. I love that folks here are not sitting around talking about their health issues, Rx and doctor appointments. Instead they are talking about their recent round of golf, their volleyball game, tennis, softball, dance classes, or planning adventures like swimming with the manatees at Crystal River, zip lining, a day trip to the beach or Disney World!"

The Villages won't be for everyone. Not everyone loves Florida, sunshine year round, tons of neighbors, and the bustle of volleyball, water polo, and golf carts. Some happy retirees may opt for a bit more quiet with a house in the mountains or on a lake. But for the Curcurus, this place is perfect.

Larry and Gail retired early and happy. And so can you.

Rick Harmon is a former executive director of one of the top 10 national Philharmonic programs. His wife, Genevieve, has been a lab process quality control manager at a major medical research institute for 28 years. Rick and Genevieve recently came into my office because Ginny wanted to figure out what date she could retire. She's 63, and Rick has already retired.

I looked at Ginny's financials and told her to retire in a few months when she hits 64. It's not worth the extra couple hundred dollars a month she'd get from her pension and social security if she waited. There's too much life to live.

They were elated. She actually came around the desk and hugged me!

What was the number one thing on Rick's to-do list? You got it—more travel. Originally they were thinking about going to live near the Redwood Forest in California, buying a condo for around $180,000. But they changed their minds. They decided they'd rather take the entire family to Australia. Rick said, "That's not a $1,000 vacation. That's a $20,000 vacation. And *that's* where we want to spend our money."

I said, "Great. Do it!"

The retirees I know who travel talk about it as a top priority for the next phase of their life. It's amazing how passionate people are about their ability to go and see the world, as if there's some fundamental curiosity inside of us as human beings to see the way others live.

Perhaps we Americans have a great propensity to explore the world because it's simply in our blood. Our country split off from England; the people who came here were adventurous and searching for something else. This could explain why exploration seems to be a core pursuit for the people in my happiness survey.

Your desire for freedom never changes. You have it when you're a kid, and then you generally sacrifice much of it while you're a working professional and parent. You give up these little bits of freedom for more money, more savings, a better parking spot, a better title, etc.

Then, when you reach retirement, it's as if you revert to being that free-spirited fifth grader again. Your priorities change. Your grandchildren are important to you—your family, your community, and the people around you, and that's why you volunteer at your place of worship—but you're also ravenous for freedom. And that's what retirement is.

Retirement is freedom. Or at least it should be.

You don't have to wake up and go to work. You've done your share of that. If it's 2:00 p.m. and you want to go play golf, you go play golf. In a way, retirement ties recreation and travel and family together.

We all want freedom. The manifestation of that desire is different for each of us, but the root of it, the base that burns deep inside, is the same. We're all searching for freedom—we just don't always define it the same way.

Stay Healthy and Live a Longer, Richer Life

There seems to be little doubt of the correlation between wealth and health. Where the debate gets louder is in regard to which contributes to which. Does higher wealth lead to a longer, healthier life, or does a healthy life allow a person to accumulate wealth?

In his article "Healthy Bodies and Thick Wallets: The Dual Relation Between Health and Economic Status," James P. Smith, senior economist for global policy think tank RAND Corporation, does admit one of his studies showed "both total household income and wealth have statistically significant positive effects on self-reported health status. This relation is only reduced by a third when controls are added for health risk behaviors such as smoking, excessive drinking, exercise and Body Mass Index (BMI) (for obesity)."[3]

This should not be taken as a definitive answer to the question, "does an increase in wealth lead to an increase in health?" Smith even says, "The causality debate surrounding the social health gradient is not a boxing match in which a knockout blow will eventually be delivered." However, studies such as this, when combined with the results of my survey, leads me to conclude the more wealth you accumulate, up to a certain point, the better chance you have for mental and physical well-being.

Following my advice may not necessarily guarantee you a healthy life, but as far as I'm concerned, it increases the odds dramatically.

Make the Most of Your Core Pursuits

Having the economic freedom to go after your core pursuits only works if you actually have core pursuits. Money by itself does not bring happiness in retirement. I see evidence of this in the happiness levels of retirees whose only income is from a pension or from social security. I believe there's something inherent in the drive to build a nest egg that has residual effects on retirees.

Smith's research touches on this very topic. He states that part of the information he studied "shows that the positive relation with good health characterizes only wage income, while retirement (pension or social security) or 'safety net' income are negatively correlated with good health."

He goes on to say the reason has to do with the fact that individuals, especially in their fifties, who receive income from pensions, social security, or safety net programs are more likely to be in poorer health, and this suggests the main causation flows from health to income.

It seems that I need to introduce James P. Smith to Nicole Walker and Meri Murphy—retirees living on "safety net" programs who are happy, healthy, and travelling the world.

The happiest retirees have the economic freedom to fully engage in their life's core pursuits. There are a lot of building blocks underneath economic freedoms. It takes a lot of time. You can't attain it overnight—unless you win the lottery, which brings to mind a recent Mega Millions Jackpot valued at more than $600 million. The chances of winning were worse than the odds of being killed by a falling coconut or wobbly vending machine. I'll take my chances that sticking to the five money secrets in this book have a much greater probability of success.

How many of the five money secrets are purely financial in nature? A solid four of them:

- Secret #2, the right amount of savings
- Secret #3, no mortgage
- Secret #4, multiple income sources
- Secret #5, income investing

Yet the very first money secret is to have a high number of interests and core pursuits. You can't have one and not the other and still be happy. **You can have economic freedom, but if you don't have any core pursuits, you'll be unhappy.** You can have many core pursuits, but with no money to pursue them, you'll be unhappy. So you have to have both.

I'm going to assume you will continue to work hard to make my five money secrets a reality. Those are long-term fundamental pieces of your happiness puzzle, and quite frankly, once you reach economic freedom, you'll have even more time to dedicate to the things you love.

Making the Most of Your Golden Years: Get Involved and Get Happy

I can't let you finish this book without a strong, clear vision of all the great things you can do with your life. This whole process is about your enjoyment. Your life. You!

Here are just a few of the things we've discussed in this book, to remind you of all the fun stuff awaiting you in early retirement. This is just a taste of all the exciting things *you* could be doing in a few more years.

Go Someplace

Some of my strongest survey data shows that happy retirees absolutely love to vacation. In fact, the happy group vacations nearly 70 percent more than the unhappy group. It makes sense, right? Who doesn't love vacations? Get yourself to the point financially where you can take more of them.

Happy retirees not only vacation more often, but when they do vacation, they spend 33 percent more on each vacation (on average). Thus, they inherently spend more of their annual budget on "having fun and exploring." More travel equals more happiness in retirement. Of course there are exceptions, but for the most part this holds true. Why?

There's definitely an element of "duh" factor here. Sure, more fun trips equal a better, happier life. It's more fun to eat croissants along the Seine River in Paris than it is to write a mortgage check. No one's going to argue that! What's interesting here is that the happier retirees see more *utility* in money. They place more value on using that money in order to get more enjoyment out of life. Hence travel becomes one way to utilize that money.

Help Somebody

Interestingly, both happy and unhappy retirees spend some time volunteering. However, **the happiest retirees are three times more likely to volunteer.** In fact, it's the number one core pursuit for happy retirees. Socializing, giving back, making a difference—it's easy to see why they like it and why they're happy.

You want to raise money to fight cystic fibrosis? You're going to have big events and parties and silent auctions and live auctions. You want to raise money for your kids' school? Volunteer your time? You're going to have events around that, and pledges, and sporting events, and Walks for a Cure, and jump-rope-a-thons, and dance-offs. There will be a lot of cocktail hour events and banquets. These are super social things.

The added bonus is that you're actually helping people. Let's say you're working the line at the women's shelter for your church, and you're giving out Thanksgiving dinner. You're physically working with your other volunteers, and you're physically interacting with the people you are trying to help.

So whether it's people with cystic fibrosis, kids who are battling cancer, women who are homeless because of domestic violence, or just helping revitalize a park in your community for the neighborhood children, you are working closely with your fellow volunteers. You're there with the people you are trying to help. There's a dynamic social environment—and that, my friends, is the essence of being a human. To me, it's such a clear, clear formula to living a happy life. Period.

I also believe that volunteering in and of itself will bring you fulfillment. I've seen so many of the lovely individuals I work with go from being a successful individual or businessperson to becoming a *significant* person. It's the difference between success and significance, and that's part of what volunteering brings out.

Close the Book

Not this one, of course—though you're almost done! The unhappiest retirees almost always reported the same core pursuit in the number one place: reading. There's nothing wrong with reading, of course, but it's a very solitary activity. These unhappy retirees like spending time with their grandchildren, which the happy retirees would applaud, but they also enjoy fishing, hunting, and writing. What do all of these pursuits have in common? You guessed it: they are often solitary endeavors.

Get Out

The happy retirees, for the most part, select activities that suggest they are highly social and enjoy being around other people. They love to give, love to explore. The unhappy group of retirees like to sit quietly and read with their grandchildren in the other room while they get ready to go hunting alone. To be fair, that's probably going a little too far with my analysis of the data, but when it comes to sewing the social fabric of our happiness, interaction with others is paramount.

Eat Steak

Not every day—neither your budget nor your arteries can handle it! But when the time is right, treat yourself to a nice dinner at one of the happy retiree spots, like Ruth's Chris Steak House, LongHorn, or Olive Garden.

Be with People

This one's so important it's actually linked to life expectancy: socializing is one of the most important contributing factors to people living long lives. We know this from *The Blue Zones*, the book I mentioned earlier.

Author Dan Buettner describes cities around the world—from California to Greece to Japan—where the inhabitants are living happier and longer. *National Geographic* even took notice. Take a look at his "The Power 9™ from The Blue Zones: Lessons for Living Longer from the People Who've Lived the Longest" and you'll find some familiar territory.

From finding a purpose and pursuing it with passion, to taking more vacations, to making socializing and family a priority, it's like *The Blue Zones* interviewed my happy retirees. It's fantastic—and further proof that you need to emulate this behavior if you want to retire early and retire happy.

As I've said, what the data on my survey and the actions of my clients have revealed is that being social is a very important part of a happy retirement. When asked directly, that wasn't a top response, yet four out of five of the top responses for the happy group, by definition, are social activities.

In other words, being social is just inherent in what they like to do. They may not know it, but their instincts do, and that's a big part of why they're happy. This just proves to me that socialization is something to strive for in your life.

And even if you are social and have social pursuits, I encourage you to continue to push that, to continue to focus on expanding your social scope, sphere, and interactive core pursuits in the world. It's very clear to me that this is a big part of landing in the happiness category.

"But Wes," you say. "I'm an introvert! Does that mean I won't be happy in retirement?"

Perhaps you'd rank yourself low on the introvert-extrovert scale of 1 to 10. That's totally fine. But even if you consider yourself an introvert, I'd encourage you to push the envelope on this. If you're socially interactive and you're happy, maybe only a 3 on the scale, you might think about ways to become a 4 or 5. If you're an 8 or a 9, I would encourage you to become a 9 or a 10. I'm not telling you how to live your life; I'm just telling you what makes people happy. The numbers don't lie.

Go Live Your Life!

I want to send you off excited and ready to find your way to a happy retirement. I think the key word here is *enjoy*. We're talking about enjoying the rest of your life!

Be like Marjorie Acton, a retired preschool teacher who took up cycling and line dancing at 65 and now dazzles people 30 years her junior. Or be like her husband Moe, a black belt in Goju-Ryu karate and former certified safety professional who golfs and plays tennis three days a week and teaches part-time at the local university. Or be like their dog, whose actual name is Happy!

Remember the following equation:

Health + Money + Social Life = Happiness

You can have all of those things if you follow the steps in this book. You can have the freedom of happiness. And you can have the economic freedom to be social and to engage in your core pursuits, the things that get you jazzed—the things that make you happy to be alive.

Continuing the Conversation

I've helped hundreds of people retire sooner than they thought possible, healthier and wealthier than they ever imagined. I hope I've helped you, too, over the course of this book. That's one of the best things about my job: I get to help people create and enjoy the retirement they've always imagined for themselves. It never ceases to amaze me how rich, exciting, and diverse those dreams can be.

If you've enjoyed what you've read here, I invite you to continue the conversation. You can find me the following ways:

- Head over to our good old-fashioned website at www.yourwealth.com. Click on the "Ask an Advisor" button on the homepage and we will get back to you within 24 to 48 hours.
- Follow me on Twitter @WesMoss365.
- Like our radio page on Facebook at facebook.com/ wesmossmoneymatters.
- Tune in to my weekly radio show, *Money Matters with Wes Moss*, on Atlanta's News 95.5 and AM 750 WSB Radio, every Sunday morning from 9 to 11 a.m. EST. You can also live stream the show by visiting www.wsbradio.com.

- Tune in to iHeartRadio. If you're outside our broadcast range, you can tune in to *Money Matters* on mobile via the iHeartRadio app available for free on all major smartphones and tablets. Just search for our call letters in the Live Radio section: WSB.
- If you're not sick of me yet and would like to contact me, check out my personal web page, www.wesmoss.com, to stay up to date on my blogs, interviews, speaking events, and all things media.

I would love to hear from you!

If the strategies in this book have really resonated with you and you'd like to speak to me directly, give my office a call at 404-531-0018 or shoot an e-mail to me and my team at wesmoss@yourwealth.com.

They don't call them your golden years for nothing. Your retirement deserves to be golden, in ways that go far beyond the bank. Settle for less and you're cheating yourself.

Best of luck to you on the journey—it's bound to be a great one. Get happy. Get ready to enjoy the rest of your life. And always remember: you can retire sooner than you think!

18 Traits of the Happiest Retirees

There are 18 traits that consistently show up in my data, and I want to share them with you here. Many of these traits correspond directly to one of the five money secrets; they may in fact be the underlying catalyst that inspired the retiree's choice to adopt these specific financial habits.

Think of these 18 traits as behaviors and characteristics—common threads that show up, time and again, among the happiest retirees. Please don't think of it as a checklist: I'd be a fool to instruct you to adopt every one of these 18 traits for yourself. Different strokes for different folks, right? But they *do* help us map out how a happy retirement looks—and they should give you some ideas of how to increase your own chances of happiness as you approach your golden years.

1. During their "peak earning" years, happy retirees average $97,869 in household income (unhappy retirees average $77,522).

2. **Current income of the happy group, either in retirement or close to it, averages $82,770 (unhappy retirees average $53,370).** As you can see in from the chart in Illustration 7.2, Happiness by Current Income (Mean), the percentage change (in more income leading to higher levels of happiness) slows down and has a plateau effect once income reaches the middle part of the happiness continuum shown on the bottom part of the graph. Economists would refer to this as "diminishing marginal returns," or in this case diminishing marginal happiness as each incremental dollar past a certain point buys you less and less happiness.

3. **Happy retirees have at least $500,000 in liquid net worth.** According to the median liquid net worth data from our survey, it takes about $500,000 to jump from the unhappy group to the happy group. The happiest retirees' average liquid net worth (different from the median) is $874,479, while the unhappy retirees average $437,500.

    However, to eliminate some of the outliers in the data (i.e., someone who reports $10 million in savings), looking at the *median* liquid net worth gives us a better idea of what level to strive for. My experience has shown there is some "psychological comfort" for families in reaching the half-a-million mark.

4. **They have a well-defined understanding of their purpose in life.** This sense of direction and meaning in life correlates very strongly with the happiest group of retirees, proving that a greater sense of purpose in life leads to a higher likelihood of being happy. The survey showed that 91 percent of happy retirees are either "very" or "extremely" comfortable with their

sense of purpose in life. Compare that to the unhappy group, where more than 89 percent report being only "slightly" or "not" comfortable with their sense of purpose. Happy retirees know what their retirement money is *for*.

5. **They have at least 3.5** *core pursuits*—**the activities and interests they love to pursue.** This is probably a big part of why they report being "very comfortable" with their sense of purpose in life. When I talk about core pursuits, I'm not just talking about idle hobbies: I'm talking about something you are absolutely passionate about, something that fulfills you. Simply put, happy retirees have more core pursuits in life than unhappy retirees—about 90 percent more. Put another way: the happy group averages 3.6 "core pursuits" while the unhappy group averages only 1.9.

    What do happy retirees do? Their core pursuits range from volunteering to travel to golf. For happy retirees, nearly all of their top activities are highly social, active, and generally involve other people. These can include (but are not limited to) travel, golf, sports, nonprofits, and volunteering at places like Goodwill or a local community food bank.

6. **Their home value is at least $300,000.** The happiest retirees own homes with an average value of $355,000, while unhappy retirees live in homes with an average value of $273,000. I find it very interesting that even the happiest retirees don't have home values that exceed $400,000 (on average). In other words, you don't need a McMansion to be happy.

7. **They don't have a mortgage, or if they do, their mortgage payoff is in sight.** The data clearly shows that happiness levels go up as mortgage balances are

eliminated. On average, 36 percent of happy retirees will
have their mortgage paid off within eight years, while
only 24 percent of unhappy retirees will. Twenty percent
of the happy group will have their mortgage paid off
within five years, while only 5.6 percent of the unhappy
group will. Hence, happy retirees are nearly *four times
more likely* to be mortgage-free within five years.

8. **They are married, not divorced.** More than 75 percent
   of happy retirees are married. Divorce has a direct
   and depleting effect on your personal finances—and
   it's typically severe. From divorce attorneys to dating
   services, becoming single again is going to cost you.
   And there's no doubt it's painful. Unhappy retirees
   who are divorced (or divorcing) lose boatloads of
   money to the arduous and emotionally taxing process.

9. **Happy retirees have at least two children (and three
   seems to be the magic number).** A solid 50 percent
   of unhappy retirees have one child or no children.
   Compare that to 70 percent of happy retirees who have
   two children or more. We all know that having kids can
   be expensive, from daycare costs to school tuition to
   Little League dues, which could explain why the survey
   results show a diminishing happiness return after three
   kids. But the results were clear: having two or three
   kids increases your chance of happiness in retirement.

10. **They have at least two (sometimes three) different
    sources of income in retirement.** These sources of
    income include social security, pension income, income
    from investments, income from rental properties, part-
    time work, and government benefits. The important
    thing is, happy retirees tend to have more diverse
    sources of income than their unhappy counterparts.
    The happy group averages 2.6 different income sources,

while the unhappy group averages 1.85 different income sources.

11. **Happy retirees spend at least five hours per year (and usually more) planning for retirement.** They've figured out the formula—unique for every individual—for how much money they need to have saved for retirement.

12. **Their spending level in retirement is approximately $53,000 per year.** The average happy retiree spends $53,112 per year, whereas the average unhappy retiree spends $43,404 (probably because there's less to spend). Note that at a 20 percent effective tax rate, a happy retiree would have to have income of approximately $66,390 in order to net $53,112.

13. **They live in the city or suburbs, not in the country.** Thirty-seven percent of unhappy retirees define where they live as "rural": almost *double* the national average (only 16 percent of Americans live out in the boonies). That's a very high correlation. Happy retirees, on the other hand, are more likely to live in cities or suburban areas, where they are less isolated and have more opportunities to engage and interact.

14. **Happy retirees hate fast food and love steak.** Fast-food consumption plummets from the unhappy to happy group, while fine dining and premium steak houses skyrocket. Happy retirees love treating themselves to a nice steak at Ruth's Chris or LongHorn. They also love to eat out at Olive Garden. (Who knew?)

15. **They don't drive BMWs.** The top four car brands are pretty consistent across the happy and unhappy groups, but the data tells a different story when it comes to the next five most popular brands—and which luxury brands are driven by each group. When

unhappy retirees buy luxury cars, they buy German luxury. BMW was the most popular luxury brand for unhappy retirees by a ratio of two to one. Happy retirees' favorite luxury brand? Lexus is at the top of their list. And in general, the happy group has a bias toward Asian brands: Toyota, Nissan, Honda, and Hyundai in addition to Lexus. Buick (U.S.) also shows up on the luxury list for happy retirees. For some reason happy retirees just don't drive BMWs, but unhappy ones do.

16. **They shop at Macy's and Kohl's.** As with cars, both groups report shopping for clothes at pretty much the same four or five major national retailers. But the real difference comes in when looking at some of the slightly higher-end retailers that were reported. Unlike the unhappy group, happy retires also frequent Macy's, Chico's, Kohl's, and Nordstrom. It's worth noting: the happy group doesn't frequent thrift stores, but they also don't shop at ultra-high-end clothing stores like Neiman Marcus or Saks. Happy retirees shop "in the middle"—not fancy, not charity—and they still look great.

17. **Happy retirees take at least two vacations per year, and when they do vacation, they spend more than unhappy retirees.** The unhappy group averages 1.4 vacations per year, whereas retirees in the happy group average 2.4 annual vacations. That's an entire vacation more each year. More travel equals more happiness in retirement. Happy retirees also spend an average of 33 percent more per vacation. So when you're doing your budgeting, remember to budget time to explore somewhere you love or have never been. Better yet, go with someone you love. It will make you happier.

18. **Their education level includes some college or above.** The survey data shows that happiness levels (in general) are directly correlated with the level of education received. For example, out of the unhappy retirees, only one in five have graduate degrees, compared to the happy retirees who reported graduate degrees at a rate of nearly 2 in 5. A graduate degree can take many forms, especially now that there are so many options: today you can get an executive MBA on the weekends or online, as well as partake in a number of other online programs offered through institutions like DeVry, Phoenix, and Strayer.

APPENDIX B

Recommended Reading

Below is a list of some of my favorite books:

Bach, David. *The Automatic Millionaire: A Powerful One-Step Plan to Live and Finish Rich*. New York, NY: Crown Business, 2003.

Bogle, John C. *The Little Book of Common Sense Investing: The Only Way to Guarantee Your Fair Share of Market Returns*. Hoboken, NJ: John Wiley & Sons, 2007.

Howard, Clark, Mark Meltzer, and Theo Thimou. *Clark Howard's Living Large in Lean Times: 250 Ways to Buy Smarter, Spend Smarter, and Save Money*. New York, NY: Avery, 2011.

Miller, Lowell. *The Single Best Investment: Creating Wealth with Dividend Growth*. Print Project, 2006.

Stanley, Thomas J. *The Millionaire Next Door: The Surprising Secrets of America's Wealthy*. New York: Pocket, 1996.

APPENDIX C

Chart Labeling

Happy Versus Unhappy and H1, H2, H3, H4, and H5

I n many of the figures in this book, we refer to the "happy" and "unhappy" groups as "happy retirees" and "unhappy retirees."

The survey categorized respondents into five levels of happiness on a scale of H1 to H5, H5s being the most happy group and H1s the least happy group. The "happy retiree" group in many of the graphs and charts in this book represents a combination of data from the two happiest groups (H4s and H5s) in the survey, while "unhappy retirees" represent a combination of data from the two least happy groups (H1s and H2s). Simply put, the happy group is comprised from the data set of H4s and H5s, and the unhappy group is comprised of H1s and H2s.

Notes

Preface

1. http://content.time.com/time/magazine/article/0,9171,2019628,00
   .html.

Chapter 1

1. Employee Benefit Research Institute, March 2010.

Chapter 3

1. www.fool.com/retirement/general/2012/10/15/17-frightening-facts
   -about-retirement-savings-in-.aspx.
2. www.ebri.org/pdf/briefspdf/EBRI_IB_03-13.No384.RCS2.pdf.

Chapter 4

1. http://healthyliving.msn.com/blogs/daily-apple-blog-post?post
   =99263c66-d36b-4a8c-ac93-50db5ed17d7e.

Chapter 5

1. Silverstein, Shel. *The Giving Tree*. (New York: HarperCollins, 1964).
2. Shaw, George Bernard. *Pygmalion*. (New York: Simon & Schuster, 2001).
3. www.bankrate.com/calculators/mortgages/mortgage-loan-payoff
   -calculator.aspx.

Chapter 7

1. www.ssa.gov/pressoffice/basicfact.htm.

2. http://online.barrons.com/article/SB10001424127887323308504579085220604114220.html.
3. www.pbgc.gov.
4. www.dummies.com/how-to/content/how-much-will-i-get-from-social-security.html and https://faq.ssa.gov/ics/support/KBAnswer.asp?questionID=1798.

Chapter 8

1. Refers only to the income piece you can measure rather than overall return.
2. http://finance.fortune.cnn.com/2012/02/09/warren-buffett-berkshire-shareholder-letter/.

Chapter 9

1. www.mhinvest.com/files/pdf/SBI_Single_Best_Investment_Miller.pdf.
2. As of the writing of this book, the rate sat at roughly 2.75 percent.
3. *The Intelligent Investor*, p. 90.
4. https://personal.vanguard.com/us/funds/snapshot?FundId=0695&FundIntExt=INT.
5. "Average Asset Allocation investors" are those invested in life-stage funds, life cycle funds, target date funds, and balanced funds, as defined by the Investment Company Institute. The 2.3 percent represents the 20-year annualized returns for those invested in asset allocation funds.

Chapter 10

1. www.today.com/id/27045699/#.UqaizGTF3Wo.
2. www.napfa.org.
3. Career Builder Survey 2009.
4. U.S. Census Bureau, 2010.
5. Ibid.
6. Employee Benefit Research Institute (article posted March of 2010).
7. Ibid.

Chapter 11

1. www.nytimes.com/2013/05/15/booming/free-from-work-and-seeing-the-world-on-a-budget.html?_r=0.
2. www.thevillagesfloridabook.com/82-cool-facts-the-villages/.
3. www.ncbi.nlm.nih.gov/pmc/articles/PMC3697076/.

Index

About the Author

Wes Moss is the host of *Money Matters*, a call-in investment and personal finance radio show on Atlanta's News 95.5 and AM 750 WSB Radio. *Money Matters* is Atlanta's longest-running financial talk radio show.

Moss is a managing partner and chief investment strategist at Capital Investment Advisors, which currently manages more than $1 billion in client assets, making it one of Georgia's largest private investment firms. He is also a partner at WELA Strategies, an online wealth management and financial education firm. In 2012, Moss was named as one of the top 40 fee-only investment advisors in the country by *Wealth Management* magazine and in 2014, *Barron's* named him as one of America's top 1,200 financial advisors.

Wes is a weekly guest financial columnist for AJC.com, the website of the *Atlanta Journal-Constitution*. As a certified financial planner, he serves as a financial expert for both local and national media including CNN, CNBC, and the Fox Business Network.

Moss holds a degree in economics from the University of North Carolina at Chapel Hill. He lives in Atlanta with his wife and three sons and loves spending time with his family and playing and coaching sports.

To reach Wes Moss, visit wesmoss.com or yourwealth.com.